MW00480306

PRAISE FOR ISResilience

I have long marveled at the ability of Israelis to face adversity and move beyond it. In *ISResilience*, Michael Dickson and Naomi Baum tell compelling stories that illustrate this remarkable Israeli national characteristic. This wonderful book profiles inspiring Israelis and their spirit, with a message that will resonate for everyone. Israel has been referred to in many ways – from ancient times as the Holy Land, to modern times as the Start-Up Nation. Now this book gives the Israeli people a new name that they have earned – "ISResilience."

Joe Lieberman
former United States Senator

The extraordinary resilience of the Jewish people in the face of adversity through every generation since Moses is one of the keys to our collective identity and sense of purpose. This idea is beautifully captured by Michael Dickson and Dr. Naomi Baum in *ISResilience* through a series of inspiring stories that demonstrate the power of the modern State of Israel, not just as a country or as the homeland of the Jewish people, but as a shining example of resilience for the world.

Rabbi Lord Jonathan Sacks
international religious leader and author

As terrorists have turned the home front into the front lines, and a global pandemic has disrupted our lives, Israelis have shown tremendous resilience in dealing with these challenges. Having served as Israel's Minister of Public Security, Homeland Defense, and in other positions of national leadership, I have seen how our resilience has been the key to our strength and success. Michael Dickson, an expert in telling Israel's story, and Dr. Naomi L. Baum have done a great service in sharing the stories and secrets of Israeli resilience with their readers, and as Ambassador to the UN and US, I intend to share these inspiring stories with others as well.

Gilad Erdan
Israel's Ambassador to the United States and United Nations

By elegantly weaving together the fascinating accounts of women and men who underwent and overcame unimaginable conflict, in *ISResilience*, Michael Dickson and Dr. Naomi Baum examine the very heart of the Jewish people's enigmatic survival.

Isaac Herzog
Chairman, Jewish Agency for Israel

ISResilience is a rich, rewarding, multidimensional work. The dynamic duo of Naomi Baum and Michael Dickson have coauthored a collection of delightful, insightful, and inspiring stories showing the charm, diversity, depth, and sheer grit of Israelis today. At the same time, they have produced a more resonant, universal work exploring just what it means to be resilient – and what it takes – which is particularly welcome during these trying, plague-scarred times.

Well written, well told, well paced, and well worth your time, this book will move you to tears – while teaching you how to "fall forwards," facing adversity with a smile on your face and a glint in your eye, mastering the human – and very Israeli – ability to overcome the toughest of challenges.

Professor Gil Troy
author, *The Zionist Ideas*

Israelis are resilient people – they have to be, since they live with the constant threat of terrorist attacks, and the ever-present possibility of war. *ISResilience* tells truly remarkable stories of Israelis whose strong spirit and resilience has not only led them through difficult times, but has allowed them to achieve remarkable success despite what seem like insurmountable odds. This is a book that will engage and inspire you, particularly during these times of great challenge and uncertainty.

Yael Eckstein
President, International Fellowship of Christians and Jews

The determination of the Israeli spirit is the theme of this book. As a daughter of Holocaust survivors, I have often wondered how Jews have picked up the pieces of their shattered lives and have not only survived but have thrived in cities around the world, including Israel. How? What makes it possible for the Jewish persona to compartmentalize pain and move forward with joy, grace, determination, and creativity? And in Israel, despite all the challenges from wars and terrorism, the Israeli spirit soars above the very real threats and succeeds in areas from technology to humanitarian aid and everything in between. Israel is consistently listed as one of the happiest places in the world to live! Why? We owe a debt of gratitude to Michael Dickson and Dr. Naomi Baum, who have written *ISResilience*, because in doing so, they have given us the gift of insight and inspiration throughout the pages of this book.

Roz Rothstein
International CEO and Cofounder, StandWithUs

Resilience has long been one of the secrets of the Israeli people. It is a characteristic that has helped this war-torn nation overcome more than seventy years of daunting threats and challenges. The portraits chosen by Dickson and Baum reveal a diverse group of Israelis who have each, in their own way, achieved greatness through grit, devotion, and a belief in the Jewish state. Their stories are inspiring.

Yaakov Katz
Editor-in-Chief, *Jerusalem Post*; author, *Shadow Strike: Inside Israel's Secret Mission to Eliminate Syrian Nuclear Power*

Michael and Naomi have penned a series of revelatory portraits of remarkable Israelis – some of them well known, others less so. What they have in common is a combination of exceptional personal drive and extraordinary commitment to their country's well-being.

Israel has not merely survived but thrived, in the toxic, precarious Middle East, because of characters like the Israelis we meet on these pages. So if you want to understand quite how Israelis consistently beat the odds and face down the challenges, while constantly innovating, questioning, and pushing the frontiers of knowledge and achievement, read this book.

David Horovitz
Founding Editor, *Times of Israel*

The stories in this book are the stories of the Jewish people through the generations. Stories of perseverance, faith, resilience. These are the amazing stories of people who took on some of the world's toughest challenges and withstood them. They represent all parts of Jewish and Israeli society and exemplify the ancient saying "All of Israel are responsible for one another." Michael Dickson and Naomi Baum have taken these stories and turned them into lessons that everyone can and should learn, lessons that everyone – Israeli or not – can benefit from.

Ambassador Ron Prosor
Director, Abba Eban Institute of International Diplomacy,
IDC Herzliya

ISResilience is a perfect guide for these tough times: a panoply of stories and lessons from Israelis, both famous and unknown, who inspire us to stand together to weather this difficult moment in history. Through a study of Israel – a country that has repeatedly held together against enormous odds – Dickson and Baum show us the true meaning of "resilience" in their interviews and teach us how we can follow the example of these incredible personalities and this remarkable country.

William C. Daroff
Chief Executive Officer,
Conference of Presidents of Major American Jewish Organizations

These stories of remarkable men and women tell an essential story about Israel: how a people that lives under constant siege, moving from war to terrorist attacks to boycotts to delegitimization, has created one of the world's most successful societies. We owe a great debt to Michael Dickson and Dr. Naomi L. Baum for telling this story and telling it so movingly.

Yossi Klein Halevi
senior fellow, Shalom Hartman Institute; author,
Letters to My Palestinian Neighbor

ISResilience gives valuable voice to a wide range of diverse voices who share their Israeli experiences of dealing with adversity and overcoming it to build meaningful lives.

Einat Wilf
author

Israel and Israelis are not always given a fair representation, to say the least. This excellent book by Michael Dickson and Dr. Naomi Baum profiles some extraordinary Israelis who – by being both tough and sensitive – have much to teach us all. *ISResilience* is an insight into the real Israel. An inspirational and uplifting read!

MK Orit Farkash Hacohen
Minister of Strategic Affairs

ISRESILIENCE

What Israelis Can Teach the World

MICHAEL DICKSON
&
DR. NAOMI L. BAUM

gefen
publishing house
JERUSALEM ◆ NEW YORK   Est. 1981

Excerpt from Yitzhak Ben-Zvi, *The Jewish Settlement in Peki'in* (Tel Aviv: Ahdut Ha'avodah, 1922) translated by Michael Dickson.
Excerpt from *Man's Search for Meaning* by Viktor E. Frankl, copyright © 1959, 1962, 1984, 1992 by Viktor E. Frankl, reprinted with permission from Beacon Press, Boston Massachusetts.
Excerpt from *The Case for Democracy* by Natan Sharansky, copyright © 2004, reprinted by permission of PublicAffairs, an imprint of Hachette Book Group, Inc.
Excerpt from *Fear No Evil: The Classic Memoir of One Man's Triumph over the Police State* by Natan Sharansky, copyright © 1998, reprinted by permission of Penguin Random House.
All interviewee photos graphically manipulated by Moran Reijzer; photo of Avigdor Kahalani courtesy of IDF Spokesperson's Unit; photo of Natan Sharansky by Ram Mandel (https://commons.wikimedia.org/wiki/File:Sharansky.jpg); photo of Noam Gershony by robbiesaurus (https://www.flickr.com/photos/30595457@N00/6128353846, https://creativecommons.org/licenses/by-sa/2.0/); photo of Margalit Zinati by Michael Dickson; photo of Chief Rabbi Israel Meir Lau by Wini (https://commons.wikimedia.org/wiki/File:%D7%94%D7%A8%D7%91_%D7%9C%D7%90%D7%95.JPG); photo of Tal Brody by Michael Dickson; photo of Sherri Mandel by Debbie Cooper; those unspecified provided by interviewee.
Photo of Michael Dickson by Jared Bernstein.

Cover design: Moran Reijzer
Cover illustration: Moran Reijzer
Typesetting: Optume Technologies

ISBN: 978-965-7023-46-4

1 3 5 7 9 8 6 4 2

Gefen Publishing House Ltd.
6 Hatzvi Street
Jerusalem 9438614,
Israel
972-2-538-0247
orders@gefenpublishing.com

Gefen Books
c/o Baker & Taylor Publisher Services
30 Amberwood Parkway
Ashland, Ohio 44805
516-593-1234
orders@gefenpublishing.com

www.gefenpublishing.com

Printed in Israel
Library of Congress Control Number: 2020912331

Contents

Michael Dickson

"I always think of Israel as a plucky little country."
Diana, Princess of Wales, to Shimon Peres,
Kensington Palace, January 1986

"We're fine."

As I write this, I'm responding to a flood of messages coming from friends and family abroad, as a long-range rocket has been fired from Gaza into Israel.

"We're fine."

It happened at 5:18 a.m.; the Red Alert sirens woke my eldest daughter first. We hurried to wake our four other sleeping children.

"We're fine."

Hundreds of thousands of Israelis were also awakened at the crack of dawn to the sound of the siren propelling them to rush their kids into bomb shelters, as I did, praying that the rocket fired from Gaza was not heading for our home.

"We're fine."

One family was not as lucky as ours was today. Their home was totally devastated by the rocket, sending seven people to hospital; it was a miracle that they even escaped alive. Cars were blasted with shrapnel, which also hit four dogs, who lay in a pool of their blood and debris on the street outside.

We're not fine.

How could we be? On the one hand, within hours of the rocket attack, schools opened, people went to work, and a normal day resumed. On the other, the conversation both in the playground and at the water cooler revolved around the attack. Yes, we are physically fine (with the exception of those injured). But mentally? That's another story.

Picture the scene. It's the morning of Remembrance Day – a solemn day when ceremonies are held and a moment's silence is observed for fallen soldiers. My family is eating at the breakfast table. My daughter turns to her sister and says, "Now remember, the siren that will sound today is the one where we stand and remember, not the one where we run to the bomb shelter, so don't be scared." She should know – her own birthday party was rudely interrupted by a rocket alert siren as she and her friends were jumping up and down on an inflatable castle, causing them to race for the nearest shelter. The wailing alarm warned all to run for cover, as rockets thankfully were intercepted above by the missile-defense system, leaving a plume of smoke in the blue sky. Meanwhile, we sang "Happy Birthday" underground, amid reinforced concrete, in a bid to soothe the nerves of the rattled kids.

My point is that the topic of my children's breakfast-table conversation, as matter-of-fact as it was, belies the stress behind the scenes. After a decade of life in Israel, my young children had known wars, kidnappings, rocket attacks, stabbing rampages, and violent acts of terror.

A tiny country in a hostile neighborhood, facing off against the rockets, the bullets, and the bombs, you could be forgiven for thinking Israel should be a national basket case. With each conflict able to turn into an existential war at any point, you might argue that Israel's mere existence is miraculous. Israel, however, does not just exist, it thrives. The idea behind exploring Israeli resilience comes from years of witnessing stressful situations unfold, of watching Israelis – both in regular, day-to-day life and in times of extreme crisis – continue on and flourish.

Are Israelis unaffected detrimentally by the threats, the rockets, and the terror attacks, the volatility of regional adversarial regimes, the ongoing potential for conflict to intensify? Categorically not. The high number of cases of post-traumatic stress disorder (PTSD) in the region of southern Israel that borders Gaza, whose citizens have suffered tens of thousands of rocket attacks in recent years, is well documented. Israel's military is a citizen army in which service is mandatory – an experience that has the potential to shape and scar both those who serve and their families. Geographically, Israel sits on a tiny sliver of land, giving national events a local relevance and impact. When the chips are down, everyone feels it.

The fact is, behind the eyes of every Israeli is a knowledge that today's reality could change at any minute. However strong the military is, you are never fully secure. However humdrum the daily routine, it can be upturned in a heartbeat. Your sons and daughters will likely serve as soldiers, inspiring in parents a combination of pride and anxiety. In such a small country, joy and grieving are collective acts in the face of national moments of pride and catastrophe. The gap between the personal, the familial, the local, and the national not only feels small but actually is small. Anyone who has lived in Israel for even a few years knows someone whose life has been affected by war or terrorism. But as seen in the immediate shift into normalcy following the aforementioned rocket attack, Israelis have developed the capacity to move on. To compartmentalize, but not to ignore. To grieve, but not to crumble. To take a hardship and build upon it – and often, in doing so, to beat the odds and skyrocket to success.

Resilience. I've seen it from driving on the roads of Israel to walking through the corridors of the powerful and famous. There's a steel to the spirit, a mettle that is just waiting to be tested. It's the resolve to carry on, the courage to continue, and the determination to succeed.

It's ISResilience. And the journey exploring what creates and sustains it was truly fascinating.

Naomi L. Baum

"Israel is this little pit bull surrounded by her enemies, and yet, it is strong enough to not only hold its own, but to flourish."
Howie Mandel, *Times of Israel,* July 26, 2013

September 1, 2000. I am patting myself on the back and feeling awfully proud that I have been accepted as a fellow in the ninth cohort of the Mandel School for Educational Leadership. I have been eagerly looking forward to the two-year fellowship, after working around the clock for more than eighteen years, most recently as director of the school psychology center in a neighboring regional center and director of the Education Department at a local teacher's college.

Who knew that on September 9, 2000, all hell would break loose with roadside shootings, suicide bombers, and random terrorist attacks that went from bad to worse in days? My dream of two years of peaceful academic endeavors literally went up in smoke, as the psychological stress of the people around me, both where I lived and where I studied, was sent into the stratosphere.

How could I sit by and do nothing? To a certain degree, my hands were tied. By committing to the fellowship, I had agreed to leave all employment. I certainly wanted my replacement at the psychological services center to succeed and didn't want to undermine her. Yet how could I sit quietly and watch the suffering of so many children and adults, as they dealt with their very real fears – and often with sudden and traumatic loss? I morphed that feeling of helplessness into the creation of the Building Resilience Intervention (BRI), an innovative project that became the cornerstone of my work for the next two decades.

Resilience, the central concept of the BRI, focuses on the strengths we all have and how we can increase them. In a situation where terror is rampant and we feel helpless, we can actively choose to focus on coping, on strengths, on the cup that is half full. Taking these concepts into the community and introducing the BRI into work with teachers, childcare workers, first responders, parents, medical staff, and more has been the gratifying result of the initial two-year fellowship that gave me the time and resources to develop my knowledge and skills in the field of resilience and trauma.

As director of the Resilience Unit at Metiv – The Israel Psychotrauma Center, I was called upon to bring my knowledge and programs to disaster areas all over the world, including Haiti after the earthquake; Mexico in the wake of kidnappings; Biloxi, Mississippi, after Hurricane Katrina; and more. In each unique location, I was humbled by the mental health needs of the local population and their willingness to learn from our experiences and practices. While appreciating that cultures and languages may be quite different from our own, I have come to recognize that human feelings are universal. Sad is sad all over the world. Fear is fear no matter if you live in Port au Prince or Jerusalem. Trying to tease out the secrets of resilience – whether on my home turf in Israel or in Kathmandu, Nepal – has been an exhilarating professional journey.

On the personal side of things, a diagnosis of stage III breast cancer in 2010 brought me face to face with the fragility of life. All of the many skills related to resilience I had spent the last ten years teaching came to my aid as I met my cancer head on. Along with this came a very personal knowledge of how resilience can assist in a wide variety of challenging life circumstances. Working with women dealing with cancer has once again been a humbling experience, as I find that I learn more from them at each encounter.

Our book, *ISResilience*, shares with you some of the secrets we have learned from the remarkable Israelis we have met about their resilient approach to life. We are excited to have you join us on this journey and hopeful that, at book's end, you will share with us some of *your* secrets to resilience. We all have them. We invite you to open your hearts to learn, paying attention to what resonates with you as you read through the book. We look forward to hearing from you – you can contact us via the website: www.isresilience.com.

The Israeli Sabra – Resilience Personified

"I always enjoy coming to Israel. Israelis are warm, they're energetic people. Forthright. Very smart. I always like smart people. They're nice people, you know. Aggressive, and I respect that aggressiveness because you need it in their situation."

Robert De Niro, Presidential Conference, Jerusalem, June 19, 2013

The Prickly Pear

National symbols can provide a shortcut for understanding national character. The English are identified with the rose. The French are represented by the fleur-de-lis. Holland is associated with the tulip. Israelis have the cactus.

To be more precise, Israelis are often referred to as Sabras. A sabra is a cactus plant, and like the prickly pear, Sabras are known for their thorny exterior and their soft, sweet interior. Israelis are, by and large, proud of this description. In his book *The Sabra: The Creation of the New Jew*, sociologist Oz Almog explores the idea that the generation of Israelis born to the pioneers of the nascent, reborn State of Israel were both tough and self-assured, a product of nurture rather than nature. Presumably, the DNA of the inhabitants of the modern state was not so different from that of their immigrant parents or their Israeli forebears who remained in the land for millennia, even as so many were dispersed abroad. Yet the net result was a sea change.

1

Israelis have needed to be tough. Located in the most dangerous of regions, Israel is a tiny country, just nine miles wide at its narrowest point. The world's only Jewish country, it has historically been surrounded by hostile states, with some bent on Israel's destruction. More than three thousand years old and just several decades young, Israel is an amalgam of the ancient and the modern. The challenges that the reborn State of Israel has faced since its inception in 1948 are enormous. These include conventional war, terrorism, the absorption of millions of immigrants from different parts of the globe, and a concerted effort by regional enemies and their global allies to malign, sideline, and isolate the only truly free, democratic nation-state in the region.

Despite constant polls ranking Israelis among the "happiest" of world populations, life in Israel is insecure. Centuries of persecution have taught Israelis not to rely on others to rush to their defense. Nothing – not even ruling themselves independently – will give them complete security, and recent history has shown them that it never will. The modern State of Israel has held an outstretched arm of peace to enemies since its rebirth, and yet Israel is unable to fully trust the peace treaties it has already signed and the others that it so desperately seeks, in a region where one Middle Eastern dictator in the morning might be replaced by another in the afternoon. Meanwhile, events play out with a critical and too-often hypocritical world judging Israel's every action. It is a biting yet achingly true characterization of the very real threats continually faced by the Jewish state that the only people Israelis can truly depend on are themselves, something they have learned from experience.

Despite trying times, and against all odds, Israel has nevertheless prospered, and Israelis have demonstrated both a personal and national resilience that is recognized by all visitors to this tiny country. You often hear tourists to Israel bristle as their expectations of common courtesy and politeness brush up against the average Israeli's frankness and blunt manner. Get to know the Israeli people up close, however, and their warmness and hospitality abounds. Therein lies the contradiction. It is puzzling to tourists, as well as to those newcomers to Israel who have grown up abroad in more courteous and considerate societies. Adjectives used to describe Israelis include brash, skeptical, questioning, determined, stubborn, hot-headed, and combative, yet those pair with warm, loving, family oriented, forgiving, optimistic, and open.

When the chips are down and Israelis feel their collective back is up against the wall, both the exterior and interior characteristics of the Sabra take center stage. Outpourings of help, volunteerism, and caring for the less fortunate soar to unheard-of heights during times of trouble. The characteristics that manifest themselves on an individual level are a microcosm of what happens on the national level. Things do not always go Israel's way; far from it. Danger, including very real existential threats, is always just around the corner. Following each terror attack, border skirmish, or all-out war, Israel in general and Israelis in particular go through a grimly recurrent cycle of picking themselves up, dusting themselves off, and carrying on with life. That's called resilience.

Resilience Defined

The term *resilience*, or as it is known in Hebrew, *hosen*, refers to the ability to withstand difficulties, bounce back after troubles, and continue on, even in the face of gathering storm clouds. The concept includes within it two seemingly contradictory abilities: on the one hand to withstand and hang tough, and on the other hand to be spontaneous, to improvise, and to dare to attempt hitherto untried solutions to difficult problems. Psychologists have talked about "mental hardiness" or "coping" to characterize the essence of resilience, but while both ideas shed some light on the concept, the true definition is elusive. We seem to know what resilience is but have a hard time defining it.

The Oxford dictionary defines resilience as the capacity to recover quickly from difficulties and adds as a further clarification the word *toughness*. Resilience is this and much more. The source of the word *resilience* comes from the science of metallurgy, in which engineers measure how much stress or pressure various materials can withstand before breaking. The second Oxford definition, "the ability of a substance or object to spring back into shape; elasticity," relates to just that quality.

While the jury is out on the "real" definition of resilience, working definitions have developed out of necessity in planning interventions to help populations and individuals to recover in the aftermath of terror attacks, war, and natural disaster. Psychological literature has pointed the way to understanding what the essential elements of resilience are.

One of the conclusions of this research is that there are people who are born with internal characteristics that foster their resilience. People who are of above-average intelligence, good-looking, and were raised in intact families tend to be more resilient. Unfortunately, these are characteristics that are not within our control. On the other hand, even those who have grown up in adverse circumstances can find and foster resilience. In this book, we have preferred to focus on aspects of resilience that people can learn, grow from, impact, and possibly control, as well as lessons that we can all learn from some extraordinary Israelis who have overcome significant challenges.

The Three Keys
The Talmud (in *Taanit* 2a) teaches us that God holds the keys to childbirth, rain (which alludes to material sustenance), and reincarnation, but leaves the rest to us. To our minds, that means that resilience is in our hands. In the pages to follow, we will focus on those keys

to resilience that we can control. What exactly are those keys? They include empathy, flexibility, and meaning. While this list is not exhaustive, these three keys, to our minds essential, will help us to analyze the outstanding people who have shared their stories with us and enable us to learn what we can take into our own lives in order to grow our resilience.

Key one: empathy. Empathy refers to the ability to be conversant in emotions, to identify one's own feelings and those of others, and to be open to a wide range of emotions. It includes the skills of self-awareness as well as sensitivity to others. A resilient person will not avoid a feeling, even if it is difficult or painful. Resilience demands that people feel a wide range of emotions, from sadness, loss, and pain to joy, happiness, and optimism. If people are afraid of pain or sadness, they tend to avoid it, shut it down, or become numb. This then interferes with their ability to feel other feelings as well. Israelis tend to be fairly open with their feelings. They show their joy and their pain. They certainly let you know why they are upset or frustrated. This empathy is an essential resilience key.

Key two: flexibility. Flexibility refers to the ability to approach life in a dynamic way. Sometimes we expect one thing and get another. Often, the road we have chosen appears blocked. Occasionally we are expecting a yes but receive a no. What do we do when that happens? How flexible are we? Can we change mid-course? Can we stop, review our options, and choose something else? Do we have a range of responses in our repertoire? Resilient people do. The famous Israeli ability to improvise stems from this flexibility in both thought and action.

Key three: meaning making. Viktor Frankl was a psychoanalyst and later the father of logotherapy, who survived the Holocaust by holding on to the idea that if you have some meaning in your life, you can withstand just about anything. He himself was living proof of this, surviving the horrors of the Shoah. Bringing the discussion of meaning to the table is imperative in our understanding of the nature of resilience. Why do bad things happen to good people? We may not have all the answers. We may actually have none of the answers. But encouraging discussion about why bad things happen, what we are to do with this, how we make peace with it, how we understand it, what message it has for us, and what meaning we make from it is essential in the building of resilience. Often, adults avoid this area of discussion or enquiry because they feel that they don't have the "right" answer. There is no "right" answer, and there rarely is one answer. Bringing the discussion of meaning out into the open is what is essential.

Ordinary Magic

Is resilience a character trait? Are you born resilient? Ingrid Schoon, a respected academic from University College, London, argues that resilience is not a personality characteristic. While you may be born physically strong, it is your environment, your upbringing, and the challenges you face that will help determine your mental capability to deal with what life throws at you, or in other words, your resilience. Resilience can be learned, and environments can be modified so that resilience can thrive. Anne Masten, a well-known psychologist who has spent her professional life researching resilient children, has called resilience "ordinary magic," a term that we embrace wholeheartedly.

Resilience is common enough to be considered ordinary. Yet the ability of people to bounce back from great adversity and continue on with their lives, often developing and thriving, is quite magical. While we have just said "bouncing back," what we really mean is "bouncing forward." This is a term that Frimet Walsh, a noted family therapist, coined to describe a resilient response. Bouncing forward carries with it the understanding that trauma and challenging life situations change people. When they return to their lives, they are not exactly the same people they were before, and they usually don't pick up exactly where they left off. Ask anybody who has recovered from cancer, survived a terrorist attack, gone through a war, and they will tell you that they are different people than they were before. This added value often takes the form of greater perspective, new relationships, deeper beliefs, life changes, and more.

Are some people more naturally resilient than others? Do you know a resilient personality when you see one? Resilient people are able to withstand very difficult and often traumatic situations. They don't crumble; sometimes they show great strength and leadership that they didn't know they had. The resilience test comes in the weeks and months following a crisis or trauma. In the first hours and days after a potentially traumatizing event, the adrenaline flows, and there may be a lot of support from the community. Resilience, though, is built for the long term; it's how people cope day in and day out when a lousy situation goes on for a while. Social support and community support are absolutely critical and probably some of the most important aspects that support resilience.

The Israeli Character

In this book, we set out to meet resilient Israelis and understand where their inner strength comes from. Our journey has taken us the length and breadth of Israel, meeting people from all walks of life. This adventure was at turns inspiring and emotional, deeply affecting and uplifting, often at the very same moment. It gave us a deeper understanding that Israel as a collective and Israelis as individuals have become particularly adept at turning a bad situation into an advantageous one – or, as the saying goes, turning lemons into lemonade.

Any Israeli could have given testimony for this book. Israelis routinely carry on with their day-to-day lives not just when things are calm and peaceful but when rockets are launched at them, through stabbing intifadas, during official conflicts and wars and unofficial waves of gruesome terrorism. And they don't just survive – they thrive. Imbued in the DNA of this nation is the understanding that survival isn't optional – it's a necessity. Two national mottos in Hebrew symbolize the hard-headed, deep-seated refusal to give up under any circumstance: *"Am Yisrael chai"* (the Jewish nation lives) and *"Ein li eretz acheret"* (I don't have any other land). As Golda Meir is said to have remarked of Israel's prowess in an ongoing conflict: "We Jews have a secret weapon in our struggle…we have no place to go."

Have Israelis developed resilience and the capacity to survive in a manner that is distinct and different from other peoples? Is there something unique in the way Israelis cope? We met and engaged with some notable Israelis to examine their personal resilience. We also explored whether personal resilience plays out nationwide, and if there is such a thing as national resilience.

Some of the people we interviewed are easily recognizable; their acts of bravery, success, and achievement are well known. Others are living out their daily lives with little public recognition, yet have overcome unimaginable adversity. Our journey took us to meet with Israelis young and old, male and female, black and white, Jewish and Arab – people with vastly different backgrounds and socioeconomic circumstances. As we observed, talked with them, and explored their personal resilience, we began to extrapolate the keys to resilience in order to learn just how an individual can identify and strengthen his or her own powers of resilience. We reflected on how these personal stories can be a window to understanding the complexity of Israeli resilience nationwide and how all of us as individuals can apply these lessons to our personal lives.

Our hope is that you will not only enjoy reading these stories, but will actually be able to apply some of the lessons to your own lives, developing your own "keys to resilience." The cactus, tough yet soft enough to be flexible, combined with a lot of feeling and a good dose of empathy as well, is an apt characterization of resilience from the Israeli perspective. Add to that a generous measure of living a life filled with meaning, and you get the essence of Israeli resilience. This is reflected in all of the stories you will meet in this book.

CHAPTER 1

Against All Odds

"If you tell yourself, 'I will win,' then you'll win."

Avigdor Kahalani

Valley of Tears

Here were the odds: Syrians, more than 1,200 tanks; Israelis, 170 tanks. How did Avigdor Kahalani, a twenty-nine-year-old lieutenant-colonel, overcome this disparity and lead his beleaguered battalion to victory, quashing the Syrian tank invasion in its tracks? That is precisely what happened in the middle of the Yom Kippur War in October 1973, at a place that would later become known as the Valley of Tears. Even today the rusting skeletons of burnt Syrian tanks remain as a gruesome reminder of an epic battle.

Forty-five years after the campaign that would define his career, Kahalani reflects on his character and what led him to this moment of extreme bravery. In doing so, he quotes a line from Shaul Tchernichovsky's famous Hebrew poetry:

A human being is nothing but a little plot of land.
A human being is nothing but the view of his native landscape.

Kahalani is, in his own words, an image of the homeland he grew up in. He was born in British-ruled Mandatory Palestine in 1944 and lived a simple life in a strife-filled region. A mere ten meters separated the Jewish neighborhood in Nes Ziona that he called home from the adjacent Arab village. Relations were tense. Gunshots would ring out every evening as night fell, targeting the unarmed citizens of Nes Ziona. Life was full of contradictions. On the one hand, young Avigdor feared that an Arab would kidnap him some night. At the same time, his best friend and playmate was an Arab neighbor boy named Mahmoud.

Kahalani's Yemenite parents immigrated as infants to pre-state Israel together with their parents. At the turn of the last century, before his grandparents immigrated, there were approximately thirty thousand Jews in Yemen. Today, after a century of persecution and resulting rescue attempts bringing them to safety in Israel, there are no more than thirty. Avigdor's mother washed floors to earn money for the family. Never having attended school, she could neither read nor write. His father completed the fifth grade before being forced to leave school in order to work and help support the family. Irrespective of their lack of formal education, the home they made together with their four children was a warm and loving one. Avigdor's father would return home from work at four in the afternoon, only to head back out, this time accompanied by his son, to work the nearby fields in order to earn more money for their growing family.

Traditions were strong in the Kahalani family. Father and son would attend the neighborhood synagogue together every Friday night and Shabbat, but there were flourishes of modernity too. Young Avigdor was allowed to ride his bicycle on the Sabbath, a practice frowned upon by some more religious Jews in the neighborhood. Unlike his parents, Avigdor, growing up in the nascent State of Israel, did get an elementary as well as a high school education, which was not mandatory at the time. His parents did not have the money to pay tuition for high school, however the Ort School that he attended allowed him to work while studying in order to pay for his education. Graduating high school in the early 1960s, Kahalani was crystal clear about his future. He wanted to be a combat soldier.

Toughness and Tenacity

To his great satisfaction, Kahalani was immediately drafted into the Armored Corps in 1962. Ambitious Avigdor quickly began climbing the ranks, becoming a tank commander and following that, a platoon commander. The journey was not a smooth one, however. Kahalani was kicked out of the Bahad 1 officers' training course as he was training to become a platoon commander. As a tank commander, he excelled, and his superiors could not understand how their number one commander had been asked to leave the officers' training. This provoked an unusual internal IDF argument, whereupon it was decided that Kahalani should return to the second half of the officers' training course, which consisted of specialized training in the Armored Corps. He did well there but could not get the rank of second lieutenant because he had never completed the first level of training and thus had not received an officer's pin. The army offered Avigdor the rank of "acting officer" and said that if he returned to Bahad 1 to complete the first part of the training, he would then get the full rank. He refused what he perceived as a downgrade and remained a platoon commander without rank for nine months. In the end it was the army, not Kahalani, who backed down, and he was awarded the full officer's rank, without ever completing officers' training.

In 1967, during the waning hours of the Six-Day War, Kahalani's army career – and his life – nearly came to an end. In some of the final fighting of the conflict, twenty-three-year-old Kahalani's Magach M48 tank suffered a direct hit and caught fire. Avigdor was rushed to the hospital, the sole survivor of the four-man crew. Sixty percent of his body was burned, and he required seventeen operations, including twelve plastic surgeries. Avigdor lay in a hospital bed for a full year. Even after being discharged from the hospital, he continued to bleed from the burn wounds, but nothing would stop young Avigdor.

Despite his life-threatening injury and his incomplete healing, Kahalani continued to fixate on the goal of serving his country. Knowing that his health profile would gain him an immediate dismissal from the army, he finessed his way back by lying and saying that his medical record was lost in the war. Surprisingly, he was assigned a new profile of 97 (out of 100), paving his way back to the Armored Corps. Just a year after flames had ravaged his body and taken the lives of his crew, Kahalani readied himself for the toughest test of his young life – getting back into a tank. Acutely aware that he had suffered a traumatic event, Kahalani worried that the trauma might come to haunt him, and he feared freezing in the line of duty.

While post-traumatic stress disorder was not a well-known entity back in 1968, Kahalani was familiar with combat stress and knew enough about the freeze response that might threaten his future functioning. He made a conscious decision not to let this hinder him. In the end, he in fact functioned very well under fire, while it was his tank that froze and refused to move.

On Yom Kippur, October 6, 1973, the holiest day on the Jewish calendar, Kahalani was twenty-nine years old. On that day, Egypt and Syria launched a surprise military assault on two fronts against Israel. Israelis went from fasting and praying in synagogues nationwide to heading out to fight a war in which the stakes were survival itself. While the Syrians and Egyptians had planned the attack for nine months, the IDF was caught totally off guard. On the northern front, Syrian forces overran the Israeli defenses within twenty-four hours, penetrating deep into Israeli territory. Over the next two days, Israeli forces were able to impede the Syrian advance at great cost in men and machinery, but the enemy was intent on advancing.

It was the fourth day of fighting, and the IDF knew it was imperative to head off a fresh Syrian advance in the Golan Heights, which, if successful, would have allowed the invading army to advance deep into the heartland of Israel. Israel could not afford to lose the strategic advantage afforded them by Mount Bental and the surrounding Golan Heights. The man tasked to counter the Syrian attack was Avigdor Kahalani.

What ensued was one of the most significant tank battles ever to take place in the annals of military warfare. Leading up to the battle, Kahalani pulled together tanks and soldiers from several armored corps units that had been decimated in the previous days of fighting. As the battle began, Kahalani directed it from the roof of his tank, unprotected. He did this in order to maintain a line of vision between himself and his soldiers. They knocked off Syrian tank after tank, under heavy, unceasing mortar fire, eventually turning the tide of the war and regaining momentum. The IDF was then able to push the Syrians back over the 1967 border, creating a major turning point in the war. With tanks on fire as far as the eye could see and casualties in the hundreds, the battlefield became known as the Valley of Tears.

Driven by Meaning

Avigdor Kahalani today is a kindly man in his seventies with a warm smile, father to three children and grandfather to seven. His final rank in the Israel Defense Forces was brigadier-general, and he became one of Israel's most decorated soldiers, having received the Distinguished

Service Medal, the Medal of Valor, and the Presidential Medal of Distinction. Had he not lied about his medical records and forced his way back into the army from a debilitating injury, the course of the military campaign might have been very different.

His heroic battle was an act of bravery by any estimation. Kahalani reflects that his courage stems from resilience: "I have medals of honor for bravery, but it's a matter of place and time and constellation. You could say that I succeeded against all odds. In Hebrew, the word *gever* [man] is derived from the word *l'hitgaber* [overcome] and the word *gevurah* [bravery]. If I had any kind of bravery, it was overcoming my injuries and returning to my tank, not because I stopped the Syrians in their tracks. I overcame my fears: that's where my bravery was." He overcame those fears via sheer force of will – mind over matter.

On the national level, Kahalani sees mandatory military service as a benefit for the personal development of Israelis, calling it "the greatest blessing a citizen could have." His view is that anyone who serves in the IDF will thereby become more mature, more responsible, more patriotic, and a better friend. Most of all, he feels that army service imbues young adults with a sense of leadership. To prove his point, he quotes the Bible: "Look upon me, and do likewise," said Gideon (Judges 7:17). Like Gideon, IDF commanders lead by example. The rallying cry of the IDF commander is "*Acharai!*" (After me!), unlike other armies' commanders who stay in the rear and direct the battle from there. As a result, more commanders are killed in battle in the IDF than in other militaries, because they lead from the front.

Kahalani compares a military commander to a stage actor on Israel's famed Habima Theater stage. "An actor, even if he has a fever, gets up on the stage and continues to act. A commander needs to be an example and a symbol, no matter what. Sure, he is also afraid, but he needs to overcome his fears."

Avigdor Kahalani is certain that what carried him through the difficult hours and days of his life is a sense of duty and a positive attitude. His way of thinking is always centered around the meaning with which his life has been imbued and the path that he has chosen: service to people and to country is a guiding beacon for him. From a young age, Kahalani knew he wanted to be a combat soldier. He never gave up, even against all odds, when he suffered burns on more than half of his body. He was driven. Driven by purpose, driven by duty, and driven by meaning.

For Kahalani, purpose in life lies at the root of his resilience. There was no finer or clearer purpose than serving his country. While it would have been very easy and even honorable for him to retire from active duty after his devastating injury, Kahalani would not even consider that route. He was a man with a mission. He would not let anything stand in his way, even a life-threatening injury.

Finding meaning and purpose in our lives can enrich us and guide us when times are tough. For many of us, this is not as simple as it was for Kahalani. Often the search for meaning and purpose is circuitous and may take us down some roads that prove to be dead ends. That is fine. The essence is that we are looking, searching, and journeying. Some of us find our raison d'être more easily than others. The key is never giving up. Finding one's life's purpose – or perhaps identifying even more than one driving force in our lives – is an important piece in the mosaic of resilience. Avigdor Kahalani's purposeful focus helped him overcome terrible injuries and subsequent fears and propelled him into a life well lived.

Thirty years since his retirement from the IDF, Kahalani feels blessed that he was imbued with a sense of duty and a positive attitude. Losing, he says, was simply not an option. He has chosen to spend his retirement educating thousands of twelfth-graders at the site of his most famous battle. Every week he meets groups of high school students who are on the threshold of induction into compulsory military service and shares with them his life's lessons. Looking across the vista on the Golan Heights, Kahalani reminds the next generation of Israel's citizens and soldiers of the words inscribed on the gravestone of John F. Kennedy, taken from the president's 1961 inaugural address. "Ask not what your country can do for you – ask what you can do for your country." As he retells his story, the students and their teachers often shed tears. Avigdor Kahalani reminds those gathered that they hold Israel's future in their hands, as he holds aloft the nation's flag, overlooking the Valley of Tears.

CHAPTER 2

David Beats Goliath

"The drug of freedom is universally potent."

Natan Sharansky,
The Case for Democracy

A Giant Mind

Religion was nonexistent in the Ukrainian city of Donetsk, part of the militantly atheist Soviet Union of the 1950s and '60s. For young Anatoly Shcharansky, that meant no Jewish traditions and no knowledge of Jewish history. He was born in 1948, the same year that the Jewish homeland of Israel was reborn, but Israel was also taboo in the USSR, as it sealed its borders to the democratic world in a quest to have complete dominion over the minds and souls of its citizens. The Soviet Union prevented any contact with the West to all its citizens, and its Iron Curtain policy curtailed movement, including the freedom to leave.

Sharansky remembers a small sculpture in his childhood home of Donatello's David with his foot on Goliath's head. His aunt had seen it at the open-air market and bought the sculpture thinking that his parents might like it because of its Jewish theme. With their almost nonexistent sense of Jewish identity, that association was lost on the young Shcharansky children. Anatoly's older brother reacted to the statue by telling his mother that she ought to make pants for the naked David. In hindsight, there could scarcely be a better role model for the diminutive Sharansky than tiny David defeating the giant Goliath. One cannot help but think about the parallel between little Anatoly Shcharansky and the superpower Soviet Union, which he would eventually help to bring down.

As we sit in his large, bright office in Jerusalem, with an Israeli flag and a life-sized portrait of human rights activist Andrei Sakharov as a backdrop, it is hard to imagine that the man in front of us once languished for more than nine years incarcerated in the Gulag of the former Soviet Union. This Prisoner of Zion (who Hebraized and simplified his name to Natan Sharansky long before his arrival in Israel) is charming, articulate, and warm. We meet in his office, that of the director general of the Jewish Agency (he has since moved on to the Institute of the Study of Global Antisemitism and Policy), but growing up in Donetsk, the only thing Jewish about Sharansky was that his father told him he was a Jew. More specifically, his father made sure that young Anatoly knew that the only way a Jew could get ahead was by being the best in whatever he chose to do. That resounding message would lead Sharansky to become an outstanding mathematician as well as a world-class chess player.

The arc of Natan Sharansky's life is as remarkable as is the fact that he brought the Soviet regime to its knees from his solitary prison cell. It was his mother who taught young Anatoly chess at a very young age. She told him it was important that he learn how to play, because in chess, unlike in the society in which they lived, one could think freely. Her son followed his mother's advice and became a chess prodigy. For

Sharansky, height became consequential in the chess arena as well; the taller his opponent, the more driven he was to beat his adversary quickly.

While these messages may have been nuanced rather than overt, there were strong undercurrents in the family household laying the foundations for the dissident free thinker that Sharansky would become in the early 1970s. His nascent interest in Israel and all things Jewish began to develop after the Six-Day War in June 1967. He became involved in the Soviet dissident movement, aligning himself with Sakharov, and as he did so, Sharansky's Jewish identity began to take shape.

Surviving the Gulag

In 1973, Sharansky applied for permission to leave for Israel. His application was refused due to "security reasons." This spurred him to become a spokesman and leader for the "refuseniks," those Jews who were forbidden to leave the Soviet Union for Israel, sometimes for months and often for years. He also represented the Moscow Helsinki Group, which scrutinized Soviet compliance with human rights. During this time, Sharansky had contact with many Westerners, including politicians, reporters, and American Jews who came to teach and support the refuseniks. On July 4, 1974, on the eve of her departure to Israel, he married his twenty-four-year-old fiancée Natalia Stieglitz (who later changed her name to Avital) in a private Jewish ceremony, itself an act of rebellion. Less than twenty-four hours later, Avital left, with her husband reassuring her that they would most definitely meet up again in no more than three to six months. That was not to be. Twelve long years of separation ensued before they would be reunited.

Sharansky was arrested by the KGB (the Soviet secret police) in 1977 and was falsely accused of being a spy for the CIA. After a six month "investigation," he was brought to trial and accused of espionage and high treason. Found guilty in the Soviet court, Sharansky was sentenced to thirteen years of imprisonment and forced labor. His captivity would include stretches inside the infamous Lefortovo, Vladimir, and Chistopol Prisons, where he spent much time in solitary confinement as well as detention in the notorious Perm-36 Gulag. Just prior to receiving his sentence, Sharansky addressed his accusers: "To the court I have nothing to say – to my wife and the Jewish people I say, 'Next year in Jerusalem.'"

In trying to extrapolate from Sharansky's life experiences some of what contributed to his resilience, a feeling of control or agency is prominent. At the very beginning of his incarceration in Lefortovo, he decided that no one could or would impact his own self-esteem. He would grant no one that amount of control over him, ever. "The only person who can demean me," Sharansky relates to us in his spacious Jewish Agency office, "is myself, by doing something that I would later be ashamed of." In Sharansky's memoir, *Fear No Evil*, he writes: "I decided it was best to treat my captors like the weather. A storm can cause you problems, and sometimes those problems can be humiliating. But the storm itself doesn't humiliate you." Once he realized this, he "repeated this principle over and over," like a mantra, until it was an integral part of him: "*Nothing they do can humiliate me.*"

Defiance in the face of isolation, intimidation, and torture became the theme of Sharansky's long detention in the Gulag. A sense of humor also became an essential survival tool for Sharansky, aiding his ability to detach himself from the reality of Soviet detention. In line with his coping mechanism of taking charge, Natan would enjoy telling his captors funny anti-Soviet jokes and watching them attempt not to burst into laughter, for doing so would betray a disloyalty to the regime. Again asserting self-control, Sharansky undertook hunger strikes to stand up for his rights and those of the other inmates.

Sharansky turned into the icon of the movement to grant freedom to Soviet Jewry, and his wife became the campaigner-in-chief, teaming up with legions of activists the world over who rallied for the cause and targeted global pressure on Soviet leader Mikhail Gorbachev. Avital traveled around the world and met with political leaders and heads of state, while Jews and human rights leaders around the world united around the effort. On February 11, 1986, Mikhail Gorbachev ordered that Anatoly Shcharansky be freed. He arrived in Israel that same day.

In exploring the roots of his personal resilience and the resilience of Israelis, Sharansky shares with us a very tight conceptual model of what makes Israel and the Jewish people unique. According to Sharansky, the two concepts that characterize Israel and the Jewish people are freedom and identity. To make his point, he says that Europe today holds freedom as an ideal, but has given up on identity, adopting the anti-nationalist idea expressed in John Lennon's "Imagine." Europe, with its common currency, passport, and open borders, has to an extent erased the notion of national identity. At the other end of the spectrum are the radical Islamists who have a very strong identity but have trampled the concept of freedom.

Central to the character of Israel and the Jewish people is the marriage of identity with freedom. This, says Sharansky, is the secret of how the Jews have continued to live and flourish outside their homeland for thousands of years in the diaspora. That, together with optimism. The inveterate optimist, Sharansky quotes a study showing that when asked to say whether today is better than tomorrow, 75 percent of Americans agree that today is better. In contrast, 75 percent of Israelis think that tomorrow will be better than today. Positivity is a core part of Sharansky's own personality, reflecting his analysis of optimistic Israel. He readily smiles, laughs, and always looks at the bright side of things. That upbeat optimism is all the more exceptional when considering the depths from which Sharansky has emerged. Yet transitioning from life in solitary confinement to life as a family man in Israel was not as difficult as one might think, according to Natan. Because he felt free on the inside and never adopted the mentality of a prisoner, it was not so hard for him to adjust.

A Woman with a Mission

When he talks about his wife Avital, Natan gets a special look in his eye, and his voice takes on a certain softness. He shared with us Avital's well-known dedication to gaining his freedom and reiterated how her simplicity, straightforwardness, and reserved nature won the leaders of the free world over to her cause. She maintained a determined posture and a single-minded focus over the course of thirteen years, never wavering for a moment. Convinced that shining a light on the plight of her husband would result in his freedom, she traveled the world tirelessly, making her case for her husband, including – famously – to US president Ronald Reagan. Yet she never let the publicity or fame confuse her or lure her back into the public eye once Natan achieved his freedom.

From the moment he arrived in Israel, despite his well-earned celebrity status, his wife Avital insisted on leading a private family life away from the spotlight of fame. In fact, she was so adamant about this that she would actually prevent people in the street from taking pictures of her husband and was fiercely protective of both him and their two daughters. Today, Sharansky is certain that this allowed them to raise their children in a normal environment and gave him the ability to live a balanced life. In trying to understand her great success, Natan is sure that her spiritual convictions gave her the confidence and were at the root of her resilience, allowing her to keep fighting during the long years of his imprisonment. She was a woman with a mission.

Avital's outspoken activism, coupled with her husband's brave stand, inspired Jews and people of good faith around the world to rally to the cause of freedom for the three million Soviet Jews. Sitting with Sharansky, the authors recall how we joined demonstrations and campaigned to support our brothers and sisters who were suffering under the regime. One of us (Naomi) was tapped along with her husband to infiltrate the Soviet Union, smuggling prayer books, Jewish history books, and books about Israel to refuseniks, along with vitamins and jeans that could be sold on the black market so that the refuseniks would have a bit of food, after losing their jobs.

You Are with Me

Does spirituality or religious belief aid his own resilience? Sharansky, who has avoided labels such as "religious" or "secular," has an attachment to his tiny, well-worn book of Psalms, which he whips out of his shirt pocket to display with a broad smile. This small leather-covered book was a gift from Avital, given to him just days before his arrest. The book was confiscated on his arrival to the Gulag, and it took three long years of fighting with the Soviet authorities for it to be returned to him in prison. The day his Psalms were returned to him was also the day Sharansky received the heartbreaking news of his father's death. The confluence of these two events led him to an in-depth study of the book, in which he found solace, joining Jews who have for generations found comfort in Psalms during times of great sorrow. He painstakingly copied each one of the 150 Psalms and then began translating them into Russian. When later on in his prison life, the Psalms were confiscated once again, Sharansky went on hunger strikes and spent more than 186 days in solitary confinement in his fight to get the Psalms back. In the end, he won the battle, and the Psalms were returned to him.

One of the first psalms that Sharansky read in prison was Psalm 23: "Though I walk through the valley of the shadow of death, I will fear no evil, for You are with me." Whether the "You" symbolized God – as the Psalmist had intended – or Avital or the legions of supporters who were rallying to Sharansky's side in Israel and worldwide, it mattered not. The idea of support, even from afar, gave Sharansky strength to withstand the worst of KGB incarceration. Indeed, the miniature book of Psalms with the tiny letters held within it a message he felt was being channeled forward three thousand years directly to him from its author King David, whose statue had adorned the mantelpiece in his childhood home. The book had become imbued with a feeling of spiritual connection and protection.

On February 11, 1986, the eve of his liberation, before alighting the plane that was to take him to Berlin and then on to Israel, Sharansky asked for his book of Psalms. He was told that he had already received everything that was allowed, and he would not receive anything more. Immediately, he dropped to the snowy ground, flat on his back, shouting and screaming, instigating his final one-man demonstration on Soviet soil. Sharansky refused to budge until the treasured book was safely returned to his hand. On his flight to freedom, he turned to Psalm 30: "I will extol You, oh Lord, for You have raised me up and have not let my enemies rejoice over me.... Oh Lord, You have brought me up from the abyss."

Sharansky was able to endure incarceration, solitary confinement, and isolation. The factors contributing to his resilience included his optimism, humor, and the knowledge that he had dedicated support from his wife and his supporters in the West. Sharansky embodied all the keys of resilience we outlined in the introduction: his fight against the Soviets was imbued with meaning; he was a man whose mission was crystal clear, and he never wavered; he knew what he was fighting for, and all of his deprivations were for a higher purpose. All of these elements together with his unique personality forged a battle for freedom that the world will never forget.

Standing on the Glienicke Bridge, which linked East and West Germany, the crossing point between Communist suppression and the free West, Sharansky's captors gave a final instruction to their prisoner: Walk in a straight line across the bridge. In his inimitable way, Sharansky zigzagged his way to the waiting Americans on the other side. Once again, David had beaten Goliath.

CHAPTER 3

Journey to the Promised Land

"For me, resilience is the emotional resources plus the social support that allow you to cope with injury, conflict, distress, and pain. And laughter. Laughter is part of resilience."

Shula Mola

A Grueling Exodus

Shula Mola and Mequnante Rahamim welcome us into their modest living room at their third-floor walk-up in a Jerusalem neighborhood that is on the brink of becoming up-and-coming. When offered something to drink, we immediately request, "Ethiopian coffee, of course!" They both smile and laugh, and Shula whips out the frying pan and measures green coffee beans into it. Within minutes, the aroma of the roasting beverage fills the air. Little did we realize that making Ethiopian coffee was such a labor-intensive endeavor, and if we had, we probably would have settled for an instant coffee. However, the wait and the pride in Shula and Mequnante's eyes as we savor the strong, bitter coffee is well worth it.

We sit on matching gray sofas in their small living room. Settling down to our conversation, Shula takes over, and Mequnante sits nearby, closely listening as his wife tells her story. Shula is completing her doctorate in communications and directs an organization for Ethiopian *olim* (new residents of Israel). Mequnante is a clinical social worker at Metiv – The Israel Psychotrauma Center – where he heads up a project to develop treatment protocols and modalities for Ethiopians in Israel. This is the first time he is witnessing his wife retell her journey from start to finish. While he has facilitated for many of his clients the retelling of their own personal exodus, surprisingly, he has never heard a complete version of his wife's arduous trek to seek a new life in Israel. This is indicative of the reticence that the Ethiopian community has displayed in sharing their traumatic journeys to Israel, reminiscent in some ways of Holocaust survivors who were not eager to share their stories until many years had passed.

Shula is a lively, articulate forty-something mother of four. She arrived in Israel at the age of twelve after a harrowing voyage from Africa, which she proceeds to relate in great detail. She has a captive audience and appears to enjoy relating her story, even if some of the moments are quite painful. In hundreds of scattered villages in the north and northwest of Ethiopia lived the Beta Israel, Jews who had been separated from global Jewish communities for a thousand years. Over the centuries, some had been forcibly converted to Christianity, but many tens of thousands continued to practice Jewish ritual, omitting many of the more "modern" rabbinic customs and practices that were simply unknown to them in villages where Jewish history stood still and existence was relatively basic. Aside from material constraints, life was not easy: over the years, Ethiopian Jews faced persecution from Christians, Muslims, and later communists.

Ethiopia in the 1970s was racked by civil war and revolution as a government inspired by Marxism was swept to power. Toward the end of that decade, the Israeli government extended the Law of Return – which gives Jews the right to citizenship in the world's only Jewish country – to apply to Ethiopian Jews. Great efforts were made to help them escape to Israel from Ethiopia, which did not have diplomatic relations with the Jewish state and which banned emigration. The first refugees from the Tigray area walked the entire journey to Israel by foot with little external assistance. Mass immigration reached a peak in the early 1980s with the clandestine operations bringing huge numbers of people from Gondar, through the Sudan, with Mossad agents waiting there to assist them to flee by plane. Escape was perilous – with the danger of robbery, rape, and disease awaiting them – and over four thousand people perished along the way. In the 1980s and 1990s, larger numbers of immigrants were brought to Israel, most notably around eight thousand as part of Operation Moses (November 21, 1984–January 5, 1985) and later over fourteen thousand in Operation Solomon (May 24–25, 1991). Today, there are approximately 150,000 Israeli citizens of Ethiopian origin.

Shula's life began in the village of Doro Wuha, a name that means "water of the chickens." Jews in Ethiopia often settled near bodies of water that could be used for purification ceremonies. Her community was so close to a river that the chickens would walk down to take a drink, hence the name of the village. One of three children, she grew up like most other Ethiopian Jews in a very rural society. Her mother, recently divorced, saw the move to Israel as a way to improve her unsatisfactory situation in the village. Despite the fact that her grandfather felt this was not a good time to make the trip, Shula's mother insisted and joined a small group of people setting out for Israel via the Sudan.

It was to be a difficult and sometimes tragic journey. Along the way, people stole their jewelry and household items, insisting that they would not need them where they were going. There wasn't enough food to go around; Shula remembers this but does not remember actually feeling hungry. She does remember carrying her baby brother on her back for many hours, giving her mother, who was in a weakened state, a break from the burden. They walked barefoot, at night, over rocks and brush. Shula can remember that her feet were bruised but does not remember a feeling of pain. The dominant emotion that she does remember is fear. Fear when highway bandits robbed them at gunpoint, and fear at the border with Sudan when the soldiers did not allow them entry. After enough *baksheesh* (bribes), they were allowed to pass through, all except for one old man who was too exhausted to move and stayed behind.

The season was summer. Heavy rains fell at night, followed by days of searing sunshine. Malaria was rampant. Shula's little brother became ill, and her mother herself was in a very weakened state. At this point, the group pooled their money to rent some trucks. They piled into the rickety vehicles, but after about thirty minutes, one of them broke down. They decided to turn around and return to the village from which they had set out. By then there was no food, and they had to beg from the villagers for some sacks of rice. Meanwhile, Shula's baby brother was getting sicker and sicker. They were at the mercy of the Sudanese, and rumors were rampant. One rumor circulating was that the Sudanese were planning to abandon them in the desert. Another rumor was that the bread had camel milk in it, which was not kosher. Starving but strictly adherent to their religion, the adults refrained and only the children ate it. A pervasive sense of fear accompanied these weeks.

Dream Meets Reality

What kept Shula going and occupied her thoughts more than anything else was Jerusalem. She spent her days and nights dreaming of the shimmering city. In her twelve-year-old mind, the goal of this lengthy and treacherous journey that she, her mother, and brothers had undertaken, along with all the other people from her village, was to reach Jerusalem. She was certain that there she would find the Beit Hamikdash, the Holy Temple, resplendent in all its glory. She pictured the Kohanim (priests), all of them dark-skinned, wearing white robes and bringing sacrifices. These thoughts got her through the long days and the even longer nights.

Shula's journey took a total of four months. The final stop was Khartoum, where the group boarded a plane to France arranged for them by the Israeli authorities, spending one night in a hotel in Paris before taking off from there to Israel. When they arrived at the hotel in France, they were afraid to sleep on the sheets, they were so clean and white. They had no idea what to do with the toilets, and when they were told what they were for, they were appalled that such a sparkling, clean, and beautiful room would be used for such a base purpose! Arriving in Israel, they were immediately given Hebrew names with little regard to the Ethiopian names they came with. Shula recalls being astounded by all the white people around her. She had no idea that in Jerusalem (and she was certain this was Jerusalem, rather than the airport) there would be so many *farangim* (their word for white folks). She had seen only a very few white people in her twelve years. She was also surprised by the immodest way the women were dressed, in tight pants and tank tops. This did not reconcile well with her fantasies about Jerusalem and service in the Holy Temple.

Upon arrival in Israel, Shula and her family were taken to a hostel in the southern city of Kiryat Gat. Adulation at their arrival soon gave way to reality. The journey had taken its toll. Her brothers and mother were immediately hospitalized, her mother for a month and her younger brother for six months. Shula's first weeks in Israel were spent in the hospital tending to sick family members. When asked how she made the journey from Kiryat Gat to the hospital, she shrugs off the question, not remembering it as a difficulty. At twelve years old, Shula was taking care of everybody and everything. Having made her way from Africa to the Middle East, now nothing was too hard for her.

After less than a year, she enrolled in a secondary school with a dorm and moved out of the family apartment. In school she excelled, and though she did very well academically, she has very mixed feelings about the school and its staff. Her feeling of being patronized, of being put down and minimized, is very strong. In the same way that she had never interacted with white people, they were unaware of black Jews. Her customs and practice of Judaism were often not recognized as legitimate or of value, and she was expected to adapt to Talmudic Judaism, without a murmur. Ethiopian culture was viewed as primitive and was looked down upon.

It took more than a year after arriving in Israel before Shula finally reached Jerusalem. The opportunity came via a school trip, and her excitement and anticipation were palpable. A disappointment lay in store for her. No-one had told her that the Second Temple had been destroyed. When she saw the Western Wall for the first time – a symbol of devotion for so many since it was liberated from foreign rule in 1967 – she was crushed. The Wall, the remnant of the retaining wall of the Second Temple, is considered a holy place for Jews and a site of pilgrimage and prayer, but for Shula it was a poor excuse for what she had dreamed of on her long journey to Israel. She had imagined the majesty of the Temple as it once was, gleaming and gold. The large stones representing its remains held no magic for her.

The Boy Who Loved School

As Shula winds down her story and Mequnante begins his, the contrast between the couple is remarkable. Shula is outgoing, lively, and some might even say brash. Undoubtedly her chutzpah and her intelligence has gotten her through many a tough spot. Mequnante, on the other hand, is a gentle, soft-spoken man, whose exterior demeanor belies his inner strength.

Mequnante begins his story describing village life in Ethiopia, as the tenth of eleven children. He was a shepherd along with his older brother at the age of six or seven and desperately wanted to go to school. His father said that only one of the boys could go to school, and Mequnante insisted it would be him. When his father did not agree, citing the brother's age as a reason to send him, Mequnante made sure that several of the goats were lost, so that his father would soon realize that he had chosen the wrong son to be the shepherd. His father acknowledged his mistake, and Mequnante and his brother switched places. Thus began Mequnante's quest for education, which continues to this day, when he is pursuing an advanced degree in social work at the Hebrew University of Jerusalem.

Mequnante's journey from Ethiopia is in some ways similar to Shula's, but in many aspects quite different. He left on his own, at age thirteen, without his family. He actually left surreptitiously, without notifying his parents or siblings, not wanting any of them to get into trouble with the authorities for aiding and abetting his departure. Mequnante joined up with a group of Jews making their way to Israel via the Sudan. His group, like Shula's, was plagued by bandits and robbers, by starvation, by trickery and thievery, and by disease. Unlike Shula, he spent close to three years in a refugee camp in the Sudan, taking on the identity of a Sudanese Arab, before escaping and arriving in Israel at the age of sixteen. There he was reunited with a brother who had come to Israel seventeen years earlier. He enrolled in an agricultural high school and spent his days as a high school student and his nights working in a slaughterhouse in order to be able to send money back home for his family to come to Israel. Mequnante tells the story in a matter-of-fact way, but considering how most sixteen-year-olds behave, he is clearly extraordinary.

Mequnante talks about the great responsibility he felt then and still feels for his entire family. Shula and Mequnante are the in-between generation, young enough to adapt to a new country and learn its language and mores, yet old enough to shoulder responsibilities far beyond their years that normally belong to the family elders. Due to their inability to learn the language and adapt to the culture, the elders have lost an element of their previous status within the family and community; they look to Mequnante and his generation for guidance and leadership. Mequnante's family eventually arrived in Israel a few years later. All arrived except for one brother, who was lost along the way. His loss is an open wound until this day.

The Fire Inside

Both Shula and Mequnante went on to serve their country in the IDF and then pursue higher education. What kept them going against all odds? How were they able to adapt to life in modern Israel, a country so different from the one they left? Aside from the obvious differences of lifestyle (starting with electricity, running water, and indoor plumbing), the move from rural Ethiopia to urban Israel was a major culture shock, which at times resulted in the questioning of the validity of their religious Jewish practice and more. Add to that economic distress and a general breakdown of family structure and traditional society, and it is remarkable that so many Ethiopians like Shula and Mequnante have succeeded. What is the secret of their success?

Mequnante is certain that his ability to withstand hardship and emerge stronger for it comes from the education he received from his mother. When he talks about her, his eyes light up. He talks about how as a young child he walked twelve kilometers (well over seven miles) to school every day and consciously hid the fact that he was a Jew. These early experiences served him in good stead on both the long trek through the Sudan and the even longer journey upon arrival in Israel.

Shula's sources of resilience were twofold. The first source of Shula's resilience is herself. She tells us that she was once invited to a group interview and was asked to bring a personal item that reflected something important about her or her life. She arrived at the interview with just herself, and when her turn came she pointed to her legs, saying that these legs of hers reflected something central and important about her. These were the legs that carried her through the Sudan. These were the legs that supported her with her sick baby brother on her back. These were the legs that went back and forth from their home in Kiryat Gat to the hospital where her mother and brothers were hospitalized, when she was only twelve years old. These legs have served her well. Shula's belief in herself, her confidence in who she is and what she can do gives her the resilience to carry on in the face of many challenges.

The second source of her resilience was Shula and Mequnante's dream of Jerusalem and the Holy Temple. This vision drove them forward and kept them going from making her way through the wilderness to long after they arrived in Israel. Even once they learned that the Temple was no longer there, this dream gave meaning to their lives; it had taught them to aim high. Though no longer physically there, perhaps, even to this day, the fire of the holy sacrifices in the Temple is burning: it is the fire burning inside of Shula and Mequnante themselves.

CHAPTER 4

Olympic Resilience

"I'm not the most talented, I'm not the strongest, not the most athletic, not the smartest and I don't have the best tactics. I think the advantage that I have over my rivals is that I take things in proportion."

Noam Gershony

We Feel You

After a tense final round, the medal is placed around the champion's neck. He shakes hands with the official and looks down at the heavy gold medal, bearing the words "XXX Olympiad London 2012," cradling it in his hand as he shakes his head in disbelief. A bouquet of flowers is thrust into his arms. He holds the flowers aloft in one hand and the medal in the other. The crowd roars out a cheer. He exhales deeply as the stadium announcer's voice comes across the public address system: "Please stand for the national anthem of Israel." "Hatikvah" strikes up as the blue and white flag climbs the flagpole, framed on either side by the American stars and stripes, at a slightly lower perch. He looks down and begins to cry, sobbing and shaking and unable to sing as the music continues. Regaining composure, he joins in for the final words of the anthem, the strings now accompanied by a brass section: *"lihiyot am chofshi b'artzenu, Eretz Tziyon v'Yerushalayim*" (to be a free people in our country, the Land of Zion and Jerusalem).

The Israeli TV sports announcer chokes up as he reports from the scene. As pictures of their champion are beamed into houses all across Israel, the television commentator says:

> It's impossible not to be with him, crying with him right now…on the winner's podium, with "Hatikvah" playing, tears in his eyes. When you look back to six years ago, at what he has overcome and his journey to get here, there is only one thing to say: *kol hakavod* [all strength to you], Noam. We are with you. We are here for you. We feel you. We love you.

As Noam Gershony moves his wheelchair down from the podium toward the cheering crowd, someone drapes an Israeli flag around his shoulders. Noam looks up at the audience and reflects; the thought crosses his mind that he is Israel's first Paralympic gold medalist. This is followed immediately by a second thought. "By all rights, I should not even be alive." That's because, by all rights, you don't fall from an Apache helicopter and live to tell the tale. You don't, that is, unless you are Noam Gershony.

Falling out of the Sky

July 20, 2006, three weeks after Israeli soldier Gilad Schalit had been kidnapped by Hamas terrorists utilizing underground tunnels and eight days since Lebanese terrorist organization Hezbollah abducted three soldiers at Israel's northern border, Noam's fateful day began. These events had precipitated reciprocal attacks by the Israeli Air Force which had escalated, as the IDF entered Lebanon to fight Hezbollah in what later became known as the Second Lebanon War. With attack helicopters deployed over the Gaza Strip and in southern Lebanon, Lieutenant Noam Gershony, an IDF Apache pilot, was very busy. This was the day that he fell from the sky.

On the morning of the 20th, Noam was assigned to a formation of two Apache helicopters and had flown to the Gaza Strip to attack Hamas targets. He completed the mission successfully. Later in the early evening, he and his copilots were briefed on the escalating situation in the north. Ground troops were about to enter Lebanon, and his squadron was tasked with providing air support. The mission started off uneventfully, but around eleven p.m., two Apache helicopters flying at six thousand feet collided and plummeted to the earth. Miraculously, one helicopter managed a safe emergency landing, but the second, the one that Noam was piloting, was more severely damaged. One of their own missiles had fired in the collision, causing damage to the main rotor. As the helicopter went into a free fall, spinning out of control, the tail rotor fell off. The helicopter crash-landed within a minute. Hearing a loud noise and rushing to the crash site to help, local residents found copilot Major Ran Kochba, thrown several meters outside the ruined helicopter, with his helmet still on. He was dead. Noam was still strapped into his seat in the cockpit, partially conscious, mumbling and bleeding profusely. He had lost a lot of blood and was having trouble breathing. The impact of the crash had smashed his lower jaw, which collapsed into his throat, leaving him no airway. The initial report from the scene: two pilots are dead.

But he was still alive. Within minutes of the crash, the helicopter of the Combat Search and Rescue (CSAR) extraction unit, also known as Unit 669, arrived on the scene. With unbelievable luck, the rescue team included Dr. Yoav Paz, a chest surgeon, on board. Dr. Paz was able to stabilize Noam, and they whisked him away toward Rambam Hospital in Haifa, a thirty-minute trip. On the way, Noam's condition worsened, necessitating an emergency landing on the rooftop of

Ziv Hospital in Safed, where Dr. Paz managed to stabilize Noam once again, before taking off to Rambam Hospital, where Gershony would remain for many long months of treatment and rehabilitation.

Noam lay unconscious for a week. When he woke, he had no memory of the crash. He felt pain and was unable to move his arms or legs. The doctors had repaired his smashed jaw and glued it shut, so he couldn't speak. An alphabetical table was brought to him so that Noam could point to letters, but since both his arms were broken, he could not use that either. His injuries were extensive. Two broken arms and two broken legs. A broken pelvis, vertebrae, jaw, left elbow, and left shoulder rounded out the list of damage. A couple of days passed, and Noam's family and the doctors slowly broke the news of what had happened. When Noam was told that he had been in a serious crash, he assumed it was a car wreck, not a helicopter accident. In a cruel twist of fate, in addition to having to absorb the details of the crash and his copilot's death, Noam was informed that separately, another helicopter had crashed due to a rare malfunction, resulting in the death of his twenty-three-year-old friend, Lieutenant Tom Farkash.

Noam expected to rehabilitate quickly and return to flying, since he had always been physically fit and into sports such as soccer, basketball, volleyball, and tennis. At the very least, he thought to himself, knowing that he wouldn't be able to attend the funeral of his friend Tom, he hoped to be there for the memorial service held traditionally at the end of the thirty-day mourning period. Now, doctors were telling him that the only way for his back to heal would be to lie in bed for two months. "That bed was like a jail cell," Noam says. His jaw was wired shut for two and a half months, and he was fed liquids through a straw. He lost sixteen kilograms (over thirty-five pounds), dropping to a skeletal forty-six kilograms (101 pounds).

Initially, Noam's attitude was positive and upbeat, but after weeks of the monotony of the hospital, stuck in bed, and in pain, Noam's mind began to wander, and he began to ask himself what he calls "dangerous questions." Why had this happened to him? Was he being punished? What if he had followed his original plan and become an infantry soldier instead of attending flight school? His parents worried about his mental state, but Noam refused psychological help. Two unlikely visits helped lift Noam's spirits. The bereaved parents of his copilot Ran and the bereaved parents of his friend Tom helped him return to the land of the living. His friends visited and played him a song titled "A Million Stars," written and sung by Tom's sister, Amit Farkash, in memory of her fallen brother; it had become an anthem of the Second Lebanon War. Those visits caused Noam to make a decision: "I will never get depressed about my new physical or mental status again, because I am alive."

Stemming from a sense of gratitude that his life had been spared and a feeling of debt to his two buddies who were no longer alive, Gershony had reached a turning point and decided with new determination to make the most of his life. From the moment they were notified that Noam was being medevaced to the hospital on life support and for the six months that he remained there, his parents, brother, sister, or best friend were by his side morning, noon, and night. Slowly it was dawning on him that rehabilitation in his case would not mean returning to his former life. The spinal cord injury he suffered resulted in paralysis of the left leg, and while the right leg moved, due to an open fracture on the ankle, he could not put weight on that foot. It became clear to Noam that he would never fly an Apache again. More than that, he would leave the hospital in a wheelchair, not as he had hoped, on his own two feet. He was beginning to realize that it was time to focus on what he could do to compensate for the abilities he had lost.

A New Focus

This new focus led him, upon leaving the hospital, to visit Beit Halochem, a sports rehabilitation and recreation center serving disabled veterans and their families. Noam tried everything, including swimming, wheelchair basketball, shooting, and more. In the end, it was wheelchair tennis that he enjoyed the most, feeling that it was the closest to being an able-bodied sport. He practiced every day and began to compete in Israel and abroad. In the winter of 2010, he was sent to Prague, where he handily won a tournament.

By September 2011, Gershony had qualified for the US Open Wheelchair Championship finals, beating one of the top players, David Wagner, the first time they played each other. Now Noam had a goal: the 2012 Paralympic Games, to be held in London the following year. The Tennis Masters Series in Belgium followed; there Noam became the first Israeli player ever to qualify for the Quad Singles finals. In January 2012, Noam won first place in Australian Open events for wheelchair tennis, again beating David Wagner, who was seeded second in the world. That was the year that he would achieve success in the Pensacola Open and the Japan Open Tennis Championships, as well as winning first place in Quad Singles in the French Open tournament. Now, he was ready for the Olympics.

London was uncharacteristically bathed in sunshine for much of the summer, and excitement was building as the much-anticipated 2012 Olympic and Paralympic Games began, but Noam Gershony's Olympic journey could scarcely have gotten off to a worse start. Upon landing, with just two days until the competition began, Noam discovered that his special wheelchair – designed specifically for his body and his needs and the one he had used in all his competitions – had been broken in transit. It was unusable. Then the draw was announced, and Noam had been pitched against one of his best friends, a British athlete who was in top form. That match began badly. Gershony lost the first set of the first match of his first Olympics. It looked like he would fall at the first hurdle. He gritted his teeth and won the following sets 6-3, 6-3. Success followed in the next round and then again in the semi-finals. Now Gershony was facing his biggest challenge since recovering from his near-fatal accident. The pressure was immense: he carried the hopes of a nation on his shoulders.

"My service in the Air Force and my training in flight school prepared me for pressure, and playing in the Olympics is pure pressure. The first time I ever actually felt paralyzed was in the Olympic final." Faced with this one-time opportunity, Gershony thought the difference between winning gold and winning silver looked vast. At the start of this, the biggest and most highly anticipated match of his life, Noam found it almost impossible to move the wheels of his wheelchair. His opponent once again was the favorite, the experienced and talented David Wagner. This was Wagner's third Paralympic Games, and he had previously won the bronze and silver medals. Within three minutes, Gershony had lost two games. Noam did not lose his concentration and ended the first set with a win. At one point during the second set, Gershony heard screaming and cheering coming from his family and friends. His opponent was approaching the net to shake hands. Noam had won the gold.

The sense of his life being a rollercoaster was crystal clear to Gershony at that moment. "I had gone from flying an Apache helicopter to being told I was disabled and confined to a chair. My military service had meaning. I took out Hamas and Hezbollah outposts; I saved lives and eliminated threats. Then I was disabled. And all of a sudden, I find myself at the Olympics, hearing 'Hatikvah' and seeing the Israeli flag. It was hard to understand how I got there. I saw my friends and family who had been with me through it all. I thought of the friends that I had lost. I'm a proud Israeli and a proud Jew. I was so proud and humbled to be able to bring honor to Israel." Gershony was selected to be his nation's flag bearer at the closing ceremony of the Summer Paralympics.

A Positive Outlook

When asked to define what underpins his resilience and positive mental attitude, Gershony is clear that while events are beyond our control, people can control and influence their perspective and outlook. Gershony, now in his thirties, is wise beyond his years. He continues: "My advice is to – on a daily basis – find the thing that will remind you how good your life is. Turn everything that happens to you into a positive." Even when he is dealt a bad hand, Gershony maintains he can twist the circumstances to convince himself to focus on the positives. Reflecting on Israelis' ability to maintain resilience, he credits "resourcefulness. We don't take things for granted. We want to improve. We always ask questions. We always ask: Why do things this way, and not the other way? We don't just accept things the way they are."

This is flexibility, one of the keys of resilience. Noam personifies that flexibility in his optimistic approach. While he had moments when his optimism failed him, his flexibility helped him to restore it. He was able to refocus and gain perspective, aided by family and friends, and most particularly the parents of the two friends he lost in combat. The combination of flexibility, perspective taking, and optimism is a winning one for Noam Gershony.

Funny, charming, and good-looking with an infectiously positive attitude, Gershony doesn't let anything hold him back. He not only scuba dives, seat-skis, and water-skis, he also teaches disabled children how to ski and volunteers teaching mathematics to underprivileged children as well. Noam travels the globe speaking to many thousands of people as a motivational speaker. "I have stage fright!" Noam laughs, "I never thought I would become a pilot, I never dreamed I would be a Paralympic gold medalist, and I never imagined that I would become a public speaker." Gershony is still in good shape and continues to play tennis for enjoyment, but rarely competitively, choosing to end his professional career at its peak. The journey from Lebanon to London provided a sense of closure, as that gold medal was placed around the neck of the man who fell to earth, survived, and became an Olympic champion.

CHAPTER 5

The Two-Thousand-Year-Old Woman

"They say I'm two-thousand years old. I was born here, my parents were born here. And we have always been here."

Margalit Zinati

Continuity after Calamity

It is an event so cataclysmic that to this day, Jews everywhere refrain from eating for twenty-five hours, from the eve of the Ninth of Av until sunset the next day. An entire tract of biblical lamentations was written detailing the destruction of the Jewish Temple in Jerusalem and the desolation that was wrought in its wake. The Temple was destroyed and the people of the capital were starved, raped, and murdered. Blood flowed in the streets of Jerusalem as the holy site was set afire. The site of the Holy of Holies, built on the Foundation Stone at the fulcrum where Heaven and Earth are said to meet, was ransacked, and the golden Menorah, symbol of the Jewish people, was stolen, never to be seen again.

A bas-relief on the Arch of Titus in Rome depicts Jewish prisoners of war laboring under that golden candelabra, an enduring commemoration of how, in the year 70 CE, indigenous Jewish self-rule was crushed by the Romans, and the Temple's spoils were plundered in a procession led by Emperor Titus himself. Hundreds of thousands of Jews living in Israel, then referred to as the Kingdom of Judea, were murdered or exiled and dispersed around the world, leaving only a tiny population of Jews in the Holy Land. The surviving Jews who remained in Israel escaped Jerusalem and Judea, moving to the Galilee region in the north of the country. They never left Zion. Among their number were the ancestors of Margalit Zinati, who serves as a living bridge between Israel's present and its past. She has lived in Peki'in from birth, a town located right next to a village named, appropriately enough, Hosen (meaning "Resilience").

Margalit Zinati draws her lineage back to an ancient Jewish family that has lived continuously in the same place since the days of the Second Temple. Throughout her life, she has dedicated herself to preserving the ancient synagogue in Peki'in and to conveying the local history and her family's story to future generations. Margalit has thus become a symbol of the Jews' eternal connection to Peki'in and to the Land of Israel, unbroken and unextinguished after two thousand years of diaspora.

Zinati, who wishes those she meets both "*Shalom aleichem*" (in Hebrew) and "*A-salaam aleikum*" (in Arabic), can trace her family back to the priests who worked in the Temple in Jerusalem. Her priestly ancestors escaped the carnage wrought by the Romans by making the arduous trek to Peki'in on foot. Once there, they became farmers and worked the land. Peki'in is located in the north of Israel, not far from Meron, where the famed second-century sage and kabbalist Rabbi Shimon Bar Yochai hid in a cave with his son. They were wanted for violating Roman edicts prohibiting Torah study, Sabbath observance, and *brit milah* (Jewish circumcision). The Roman leaders, intent on wiping out Jewish practice and the Jewish people, sentenced many of the leading rabbis to death, including Rabbi Shimon Bar Yochai.

Legend tells that a carob tree grew up miraculously right next to the cave where he and his son were hiding and provided them with food, and a spring appeared to give them water to drink as well as a mikveh (ritual bath) in which to immerse themselves. It was there, according to tradition, that Rabbi Shimon Bar Yochai wrote the *Zohar*, the foundational book of the Jewish mystical tradition. The site is considered holy by many, and the nearby natural spring and ancient carob tree can be visited even today.

Visiting Zinati, one needs to listen carefully, as she talks in Hebrew with an Arabic accent. Her deeply lined face reflects the many years she has walked this earth and all she has seen and experienced. Zinati speaks of the town's synagogue, whose building included two ancient stones brought from the Temple itself by her ancestors. One stone depicts the seven-branched Temple Menorah, the lulav and etrog used on the Sukkot festival (Tabernacles), and the shofar (ram's horn), as mentioned in the Bible. On the other side facing it is a stone featuring an illustration of the Nicanor Gate, one of the seven gates of the Temple courtyard. In today's synagogue, the stones are situated opposite each other, but originally, they were placed face down as a way to acknowledge the devastation of the destruction of the Temple. Only when the modern-day State of Israel gained its independence were the stones once again placed upright, says Margalit, to symbolize that Israel would last forever. "The people of Israel never left their homeland," Zinati declares, "and I hope that they will never leave. I am the keeper of the flame. I'm here, keeping the embers of Jewish presence in Peki'in alive."

Coexistence and Conflict

In the eleventh century, Arabs joined the Jewish residents of Peki'in, who were followed by Christians in the twelfth century and Druze in the eighteenth century. Peki'in became a model of coexistence. The second-largest Greek Orthodox Church in Israel was built there in 1894. Zinati speaks fondly of the Jewish festival of Simchat Torah, the holiday on which Jews rejoice in the completion of the Torah reading cycle. This Jewish holiday became a special celebration for everyone. Local Christians, Druze, and Muslims would wish each other *chag sameach* (happy holiday) and dance with the Jews and their Torah.

The communities lived together. During Passover, the local Jews would provide those of other faiths with matzah, and as the holiday ended, the non-Jews would bring pita (pocket bread) to their Jewish neighbors. Weddings, like the holidays, were celebrated by all. Nowadays, Peki'in is populated by several thousand Druze. Margalit is the only remaining Jew in Peki'in. Over the centuries, Israel was occupied and reoccupied by different rulers, yet the Zinati family persevered in the town of Peki'in. The Jews of Peki'in are mentioned by Rabbi Moses Basola, a traveler who arrived in Peki'in during Passover in 1522. He published a book about his travels, leaving a record that substantiates Margalit's family story.

First the Romans, then the Byzantines, the Arabs, the Crusaders, the Mamluks, the Ottomans, and then the British all took a turn controlling this special piece of land. The various rulers all had an impact on the local residents. Zinati's family, like their Jewish neighbors, became Mustarabim – Jews heavily influenced by Arab culture – and began taking on Druze modes of dress and speaking Arabic. However, the Jews of Peki'in maintained an unwavering commitment to Jewish rites and rituals.

The town hosted a seminal visit in 1922, when Zionist leader and future president of Israel Yitzhak Ben-Zvi arrived in Peki'in. Ben-Zvi became a patron of the town and later was instrumental in the Israeli government's interest in investing in and maintaining the heritage sites of Peki'in. Ben-Zvi was so impressed with his visit to Peki'in that he wrote a book about his visit (*The Jewish Settlement in Peki'in*) in 1922. He wrote:

> Like an ancient legend, and like an echo rising up from the depths of centuries, awareness of the remnants of the Jewish peasant farmers rings in our ears.... Peki'in is not beyond the rivers of Kush, but here among us.

Ben-Zvi arranged for the renovation of the cemetery and synagogue and inspired a reawakening among the local Jews. Margalit credits Ben-Zvi for reminding her family of their Jewish roots following decades of Arab influence, and she proudly holds aloft the modern-day 100-shekel bill with a picture of President Ben-Zvi on one side and an illustration of the door and window of Peki'in's synagogue on the other.

While coexistence was often the order of the day, Peki'in has known more difficult times. In 1936, the Arab Revolt led by Grand Mufti Haj Amin al-Husseini began. Hundreds of Jews were killed and injured throughout the land. Husseini, who later became infamous for meeting with and professing friendship for Hitler, was eager to put an end to Jewish immigration in British-mandated Palestine. It took three years to crush the violent protests, but the net result was the British caving in to the violence and the creation of the White Paper of 1939 drastically limiting the number of Jews allowed to immigrate legally to British Mandate Palestine. During this time, the Jews of Peki'in found themselves, like many of their brothers and sisters across the country, in the crosshairs of violent Arab attacks. Margalit recalls when her father was nearly murdered. He was about to be doused in kerosene and set alight in public by the attackers when a Muslim neighbor intervened and saved his life. Most Jews fled the town during the violence of those years. After quiet returned to the village, the Zinati family were the only Jewish family who came back.

Keeper of the Flame

With no children of her own, Margalit cared for her parents, and after they passed away, her primary concern was preserving the Jewish roots of her hometown. She faithfully takes the keys to the synagogue, each and every day, opens it up, cleans it, and ensures its upkeep. She personally welcomes all visitors to the site of the synagogue, right next to the one-bedroom home she was raised in. In 2018, on the seventieth anniversary of the creation of the modern state, Margalit Zinati was fittingly honored. The "keeper of the flame" was chosen to light one of the Independence Day torches at the prestigious national ceremony in Jerusalem. Despite her advanced years, she has played a daily role in personally hosting groups at the Beit Zinati (House of Zinati) Visitors' Center in Peki'in, a charming and fascinating off-the-beaten-track place to visit.

It took almost two thousand years for the Jewish commonwealth to be reestablished in the Land of Israel in May 1948. The Menorah, whose theft from the Holy of Holies in the year 70 CE is celebrated on the Arch of Titus, was chosen as the official symbol of the modern State of Israel. Peki'in is a testament to continuous, uninterrupted Jewish presence in the Land of Israel from time immemorial. Whereas today, Jews are so often described in terms of where they were exiled to or where their family was living most recently, or by whether they are Ashkenazi or Sefardi/Mizrachi, Margalit Zinati and her family demonstrate that these are modern, artificial constructs and that all Jews trace their roots back to the place that her family never left: the Land of Israel. The story of the Jewish people in Israel persevering from the time of the destruction of the Temple until now is one of sustained determination, overcoming hardship and persecution in order to survive and thrive.

Jews are the People of the Book, and Jewish survival has been perpetuated by their ability to tell their story. No one is more personally emblematic of that story than Margalit Zinati. Margalit still regales spellbound audiences who visit the town of Peki'in with stories of the glory of days past. She no longer has any living relatives, so the many thousands and even tens of thousands who have met her will carry Zinati's torch as they tell future generations about the two-thousand-year-old woman.

CHAPTER 6

From the Ashes

"We have no choice! We are not fighting for status, prestige, or ego. We are fighting for our lives. We are fighting for our country. We have no other country! This is it. We have no choice."

Rabbi Israel Meir Lau

Where They Don't Kill Jews

Sitting in Rabbi Israel Meir Lau's formal living room, it is hard to imagine this venerable elder, immaculately dressed in a black satin frock coat, sporting a long white beard and twinkling eyes, as an eight-year-old orphan and three-year veteran of Buchenwald concentration camp. As he shares with us his bone-chilling stories of seeing his father murdered, being torn from his mother's arms at age five, and getting tossed into a cattle car with his sixteen-year-old brother, it is unfathomable that someone so young could have experienced such horrors and not only lived to tell the tale, but gone on to become one of the foremost spiritual leaders of Israel today.

When asked to reflect about how the Holocaust shaped him and affected the State of Israel today, Rabbi Lau replies that this is a redundant question. The devastating attempted genocide murdered over a third of the world's Jewish population. Despite some political opposition from many quarters, that this had been allowed by the nations to occur was an important part of the moral case for the rebirth of an independent Jewish country. For Rabbi Lau, it is clear that the Holocaust loomed large as an independent Israel was reestablished in 1948. It is not purely because of the Holocaust that there is an Israel, but had there been an Israel at the time, the Holocaust could not have taken place. Indeed, it was this thought – that Israel is a place where Jews are not killed – that kept him going as a child surviving the Holocaust.

Sitting in a relaxed setting on a sofa in his Tel Aviv home, Rabbi Lau shares with us his incredible biography. While he has probably told his story thousands of times and has written extensively about it, most notably in his autobiography, *From the Ashes*, retelling it does not fail to stir him and bring very real tears to his eyes. We ask him about his arrival as one of the first postwar immigrants to the Promised Land. Listening to him vividly retell how his ship, carrying orphan refugees, landed on the shores of British Mandate Palestine in 1945, one can picture the scene of his entry.

He tells us how his brother had gone off to find their belongings as they neared the shore, and the man whom he was with told him that the men rowing their boats out to the large ship to bring passengers to shore were Arabs. He scared the eight-year-old Lau, who – even at this young age – had more than a lifetime's experience of horror and fear, joking that the reason the Arabs wore *sharwal* (wide pants that drooped down in the middle) was to hide the Jewish children they kidnapped. Yisrael started screaming and bawling, telling his brother that he would not get off the ship. It took several long minutes for Naphtali, Yisrael's nineteen-year-old brother, to understand what had happened when he left his brother's side, and longer until he was able to calm his brother down and explain that the man was just teasing him, and that in fact the Arabs would not kidnap him.

But to little Yisrael, or Lulek, as he was known in Yiddish, this was no joking matter. He was a boy carrying an unbearable weight on his shoulders. He knew no Hebrew and nothing about Israel. He was unschooled and unlettered, having spent his childhood years in the ghetto of Piotrków, forced into slave labor at the age of six in the Hortensia Glass Factory and then in the inconceivable horrors of Nazi concentration camps. The only thing he knew was what his brother Naphtali – also known as Tulek – had told him: *Israel is the place where they don't kill Jews.* Unimaginable! There was actually a place in this world where they didn't kill Jews? Eight-year-old Lulek could not even conjure up what that might look like. His brother Naphtali had become his guardian and sole support on that awful day in late 1944 when the ghetto was liquidated. At the train station, on a crowded platform filled with Nazis, their dogs, and frightened Jews, his mother made the split-second decision to push him to Naphtali's group with the men, realizing that the women and children would meet with certain death.

After spending several months in a forced labor camp, they were transported to Buchenwald, arriving in mid-winter, at the outskirts of Weimar, cradle of German culture, the birthplace of Goethe and Schiller. Understanding that Lulek's only chance to survive the death camp was to pretend he was Polish, his brother Naphtali was able to procure for him the letter *P* and sewed it onto his uniform in place of the *J* for Jew. Within days, he was transferred to Block 8, where Russian prisoners were held. Better food and easier work ensured that seven-year-old Lulek would have a chance at survival. The men of the block adopted him, and though the separation from Naphtali was excruciating, his brother was insistent and gave him no choice. He explained to Lulek that he must pretend that he was not Jewish, and the youngster immediately agreed, understanding innately that his life depended on this.

Despite the separation, Naphtali would drag himself up to the fence separating him from his younger brother every few days to make sure he was okay. Never for a moment did he forget his mother's charge to him that day on the platform when she pushed Lulek into Naphtali's arms, saying "Tulek, take care of Lulek." Nor did he forget his father's charge to make sure the family's rabbinic lineage would be perpetuated. Meanwhile, the Nazis assigned to Naphtali the most indescribably horrible job of carting bodies from the gas chambers to the crematoria.

Naphtali became what the inmates referred to as a Musselmann, one who is on the verge of starving to death. Few survived. As rumors ran rampant, with prisoners fearing that the Germans would kill them all before the Americans or Russians could liberate them, an emaciated Naphtali dragged himself over to the fence by Block 8 once more and called to Lulek, who ran out to see his beloved brother. With tears in his eyes, Naphtali told him that if they should ever be separated, and if the war should one day be over, he, Lulek, should go to Eretz Yisrael (the Land of Israel). Lulek had no idea what that was. He knew no Hebrew. He hardly remembered a thing about Jewish practice. The one thing he knew was how to survive. His brother made him repeat the words over and over: Eretz Yisrael, the Land of Israel, Eretz Yisrael. Lulek had only one question for his brother. "*Czemu?*" he asked in Polish. "Why?" Why had his brother told him to go to Eretz Yisrael, and only to Eretz Yisrael? *Because there, they don't kill Jews.*

The Unbroken Chain

Some seventy-five years later, in the living room of his stately Tel Aviv home, Rabbi Lau repeats the phrase: *Here, they don't kill Jews.* Luckily, he was not, in the end, separated from Naphtali. He goes on to describe the trials and travails of coming to Israel in July 1945 as an eight-year-old orphan and Holocaust survivor. He highlights the wonderful care he received from his aunt and uncle, who had moved to Kiryat Motzkin, a suburb of Haifa, before World War II. Yisrael Meir's uncle explained to him that he had been saved in order to realize his destiny: to follow in the footsteps of his esteemed rabbinic family, succeeding his late father to become the thirty-eighth generation in an unbroken family chain of rabbis. This is exactly what he did, immersing himself in Torah study in various yeshivot (institutions of higher Torah learning). In each yeshiva he found a mentor, someone who knew his father, Rabbi Moshe Chaim Lau, the last chief rabbi of their Polish town of Piotrków Trybunalski, who was murdered in the Treblinka extermination camp. Yisrael Meir Lau, in winning fashion and with inestimable charisma, was able to make bonds and bring out the best in people, who wished to help this young orphan with the most incredible life experiences to pursue his dream of perpetuating the esteemed line of rabbinic and spiritual leaders.

Naphtali, Rabbi Lau's older brother, took his father's charge most seriously to make sure that the rabbinic dynasty of their family would continue. Rabbi Lau relates that in 1993, when he was appointed chief rabbi of Israel, he and his brother went to the Western Wall to offer up thanks to the Almighty. His brother then turned to the new chief rabbi and said to him that only now did he feel he had been relieved of a great weight. For the last fifty years, he had been walking around with the burden that his father had placed on him on that fateful day in 1942. Now that Lulek had become the chief rabbi of Israel, he could rest easy.

In considering the path he has chosen to take, Rabbi Lau most vehemently states that he has chosen life, he has chosen ambition and opportunity to fuel his achievements. Yes, life dealt him unimaginably difficult blows, but giving in to them would have given victory to the Nazis. His conscious response to fear, deprivation, and feeling alone in the world was to seek out every opportunity, to relish every kind word or response, and to use his great gifts to make his mark on the world.

Rabbi Lau notes that his father was a renowned public speaker, and often over the course of the years, people who had the opportunity to hear his *derashot* (Torah discourses) would come over to Rabbi Lau to tell him how powerful they were and what an impact they had made. Rabbi Lau has continued in that tradition and is a powerful charismatic orator, with a very simple message: The Jewish people must continue. Jewish tradition is at the very heart of our lives here in Israel, the country in the world *where they don't kill Jews*.

Rabbi Lau's ability to rise from the ashes and achieve all that he has accomplished in his lifetime is remarkable. In considering what contributed to Rabbi Lau's resilience in the face of the devastation and loss he experienced at such a young age, one cannot overlook his early beginnings and the very strong bonds he had with his parents – and particularly with his mother – during the first five years of his life. Rabbi Lau tells how his mother made sure to bring his favorite honey cookies with them to the hiding place where they were escaping the Gestapo, in order to make sure the four-year-old Lulek wouldn't make any noise at the wrong moment. Her ability to be in tune with her son and to understand his needs despite her own worries and anxiety is indicative of masterful parenting. Studies show that early attachment is key in later psychological development, and solid, stable attachment to parental figures helps form a strong core in youngsters. If parenting is inadequate, if children are abused or neglected, this may have far-reaching implications for their future ability to cope and weather the challenges of life. Although he lost them at far too young an age, little Lulek was fortunate indeed to be born to the parents he had.

Not only did his mother and father lay the foundation for Yisrael Lau's resilience, but also his brother Naphtali was a key player. His brother kept him close, protecting him under extraordinary conditions, and did not give up on him for a moment, even though his own life undoubtedly would have been simpler without the burden of being the guardian of a child. His brother Naphtali stood in for mother and father, sheltering the young Lulek as best he could.

Bringing Out the Best in Others

Trying to picture the seven-year-old Yisrael Meir Lau in the Buchenwald death camp, in the special block Naphtali was able to get him into that was reserved for non-Jewish Russian and Polish political prisoners, one can only imagine that he had a lot of presence and charm, even then. Studies bear out that children who are winning, who are able to communicate and to attach themselves to adults in their environment – to find mentors and protectors – are more successful in life. Lulek found love and protection from one Russian prisoner in particular, who not only gave him larger food portions, but also covered Lulek's body with his own, when during the final battle before liberation, bullets whizzed overhead from all directions. Until this day, Rabbi Lau is certain that the Russian prisoner Feodor Mikhailichenko is the one who saved his life. Seventy years later, Rabbi Lau made a special visit to Rostov, Russia, to pay his respects at the grave of his rescuer.

Upon arriving in Israel, the eight-year-old was fortunate to reconnect with his aunt and uncle, who brought him into their family and treated him as a beloved son. These wonderful people, who were barely making ends meet as it was, unhesitatingly provided him with all his material and emotional needs during his first years in Israel. One can only imagine that this was not an easy task. As Yisrael Meir Lau grew up, he left his aunt and uncle's home to attend a yeshiva in Jerusalem. The rabbis and teachers he met were also charmed by him and taken by his personal story and his personality. He felt cared for and appreciated the special interest that the adults he met took in him. Everywhere he went, he seemed to bring out the best in people.

Having witnessed unspeakable horrors, Rabbi Lau built upon those tragic foundations to marry Chaya Ita Frankel, the daughter of Rabbi Yitzchak Yedidya Frankel, chief rabbi of Tel Aviv-Jaffa, and to create a home and raise a family of his own – three sons and five daughters. He was able to dedicate his life to serving his communities, as chief rabbi of the coastal city of Netanya and then of Tel Aviv, and subsequently chief rabbi of all of Israel. Rabbi Lau became a well-known leader in Israel and on the global scene, meeting with world leaders and winning both the Israel Prize and the French Legion of Honor, the former recognizing his contribution to the State of Israel and the latter acclaiming his work building bridges between different religions.

In January 2020, a historic event took place. Forty-seven global leaders, among them presidents, prime ministers, and members of royal families, gathered together at Yad Vashem World Holocaust Remembrance Center in Jerusalem to commemorate the seventy-fifth anniversary of the liberation of Auschwitz concentration camp. It was an extraordinary spectacle, and many moving speeches were given, but perhaps the most poignant moment belonged to the man representing the Holocaust survivors at the state ceremony, Rabbi Lau. He addressed the audience in his rabbinic garb, speaking forcefully, yet with quiet restraint. "I cannot forgive, because I'm not authorized to forgive. My parents, before they went away, before they were *taken* away, they did not ask me to forgive. They asked me to continue the chain, so the Jewish chain will be unbroken, unbroken forever. That's what they said. My mother…[said], 'Remember that you are a Jew, wherever you go, remember you are a part of a rabbinic chain…' She didn't speak about forgiveness. What else do you ask me? To forget. Forget? How can I forget? How can I forget the beatings, the freezing, the starvation?… I do remember the sufferings. I do remember the tortures. I do remember the victims. And I can never forget."

Rabbi Israel Meir Lau is a man with a mission. It was ever thus. At a young age, he was commanded to survive in order to get to Israel. Soon afterwards, the raison d'être instilled in him from childhood was to carry on the family rabbinic tradition. Having a sense of mission kept him alive during the Holocaust and guided all his steps during his formative years. This mission has been a beacon to him his entire life – a strong and clear purpose that was an essential part of Rabbi Lau's resilient climb from the ashes of the Holocaust to the Chief Rabbinate of the modern State of Israel. Now in his eighties – impressive, energetic, and forward-looking – he has as keen a sense of loss as ever, but he can now say to his younger self: mission accomplished.

CHAPTER 7

Glass Ceilings

"Stay focused. When the door was closed on me, I found other doors."

Gadeer Kamal-Mreeh

Bridging Realities

The phone rang, and Gadeer Kamal-Mreeh answered it. It was a short conversation but enough to bring her to tears. The voice on the other end of the line was Sheikh Muafak Tarif, spiritual leader of the Israeli Druze community. He congratulated her on becoming Israel's first female Druze member of Knesset and told her how proud he was of her. To understand Gadeer's tears, it is important to understand the barriers she broke, the community from which she had come, and the obstacles that were in her way along the road to reaching the Knesset, Israel's parliament.

It is hard to imagine that any of this was actually so difficult, when we meet Gadeer (pronounced "Ra-deer") at her parliamentary office inside Israel's Knesset. A gold sign sits on a teak desk with the words "Boss Lady" imprinted on it. She is dressed in pressed slim jeans and a silk blouse, and her office is adorned with an Israeli flag proudly standing in the corner. Gadeer Kamal-Mreeh has blazed her own trail to arrive at the place where she is today.

Gadeer was born and raised in Dalyat al-Karmel, a Druze village established in the seventeenth century that has grown into a town located south of the city of Haifa. This is where her parents and grandparents were born as well. Her father, a builder, imbued in her the message that if you want to succeed, you will succeed. He told her that she could achieve anything she wanted and that the sky was the limit. As a child, Gadeer had a dream and a direction. She knew that someday she would be a TV journalist and used to practice with a microphone looking into the mirror, pretending that she was on prime time. While she was determined to reach her goal, the journey toward her aspirational objective was anything but straight or clear. Gadeer's community, the Druze community of Israel, which numbers approximately 140,000, is situated at a particularly special and sensitive part of Israeli society. The Arabic-speaking Druze are a unique ethnoreligious minority in Israel. Their religion dates back to the tenth century when they broke away from mainstream Islam. Although their rituals and beliefs are kept secret, it is known that Druze believers recognize the prophets of Islam, Christianity, and Judaism. Their most revered prophet is Jethro, the father-in-law of Moses.

While hundreds of thousands of Druze live in Lebanon and Syria, and some in Jordan as well, they disavow greater Arab nationalism, and their loyalty lies with the country in which they reside. Interestingly, the Druze have their own five-colored flag, each color symbolizing one of their prophets, yet their respect for the blue-and-white national flag of Israel, emblazoned with a Star of David, is total. Gadeer explains that to the Druze, land is secondary, and loyalty to their country of birth is of primary importance. As far back as 1948, the Druze community has shown this loyalty, fighting bravely and falling alongside their Jewish countrymen in the War of Independence. Druze were accepted as full citizens from the inception of the modern State of Israel. In 1956, the mandatory military conscription law was passed, and Druze males have been drafted into the IDF ever since, unlike their Muslim counterparts, who are exempted from the draft but can choose to volunteer. Historically, many Druze have achieved high-ranking positions in the army.

Gadeer maintains that the experience of being a minority community in Israel has positive elements and that other minorities could learn a lot from the Druze experience. She says that from an early stage in the creation of the modern State of Israel, the Druze leadership understood the similarity between Druze and Jews and their mutual interests. They recognized that the democracy that would be established in 1948 would be good for their community, and they understood the importance of serving in the army to defend the country they call their own.

For Gadeer this dual identity, Israeli and Druze, is something to cherish, and she feels that her community has been successful in bridging the two realities. She makes the intricacies of melding various identities sound so easy and matter-of-fact. "On the one hand," she says, "we have our own religious identity, and on the other we live in the big, wide world. We are conservative and liberal. We are West and East. We have our own flag, but we know that our flag is the Israeli one. I am an anchorwoman, a journalist, a member of Knesset, and a simple Druze woman who can learn from her mother-in-law how to cook traditional dishes – all these factors enrich us and enrich my identity."

In fact, while balancing these diverse facets of life is a beautiful thing, it is also a daily challenge, and one that is even harder for women than men. Women often face more difficulties on the road to success, and Druze women are no exception. Women in the Druze community are expected to be modest and private people, whose focus is on the home and family. Gadeer's mother was a traditional Druze homemaker, dedicating all her time and energy to her family. Gadeer has tremendous respect for her mother and the standards that she set. Looking at her own life, Gadeer is always trying to find a balance between career and family, like so many others of her generation.

Breaking Through

Soon after starting out in her journalistic career, Gadeer was given the opportunity to anchor a television show, an Arabic-language program about social issues. The show was a success, as was Gadeer, and in 2017 she was offered a new and exciting opportunity that would thrust her into the public spotlight. She was chosen to anchor the prime-time Hebrew-language evening news on Israel national television. While Gadeer was thrilled with this high-profile, breakthrough position, what followed was pushback from her community. Religious leaders lobbied her parents, saying that this role was not appropriate for a Druze woman because it was so visible and furthermore required long hours away from home. Gadeer felt isolated and lonely, censured by many in her community for the choice she was making. Gadeer recalls being stopped in the street and strongly admonished by a neighbor. The easy option at this point would have been to pull back and take another path, but she was not deterred. In fact, her biggest fans were her mother, father, and husband, who bolstered her flagging confidence and supported her throughout.

There is more to reading the evening news than just sitting facing the camera in the news studio wearing TV makeup. Gadeer's day began early and required her to be fully up to speed on the intricacies of Middle East politics and Israeli society. She needed to be on top of things in a country where news breaks around the clock and where war can begin and regimes can fall by the end of a day. Soon, she recognized a subtle shift in the perception of her by her own community. Slowly, her new on-air presence became respected and embraced. Since that time, Gadeer credits her community and in particular her family for giving her the strength and support she needs to succeed. As she notes, "It takes a village to raise a child," and she is very fortunate to have that village helping her on a daily basis.

Another challenge Gadeer has had to contend with is geography. Living in the periphery of Israel means that everything from education to local resources to distances from the main population centers is more demanding than living in Tel Aviv or Jerusalem, where her TV studio was located. It often takes upward of two hours to reach her office in the Knesset, and of course the return trip awaits her at the end of the day.

Gadeer's husband, a successful businessman in medical technology, is also Druze, and also from Dalyat al Carmel. She met him in an online chat room, and as fate would have it, they are distant relatives, even though they had never met before. When they married, Gadeer was in her early twenties. They have two young boys. Her husband is very supportive, helpful, and always encouraging. She depends on her extended family not only for babysitting, but primarily to share the burden and the joy of raising her two sons. When asked directly about what is at the core of her personal resilience and inner strength, she points unhesitatingly to her very strong sense of belonging, starting with the inner circle of her family and moving on to the community. Without question, these rings of support are the basis of her inner steel to push on and succeed.

Who among us has achieved our life's dream and ambition by age thirty? Gadeer certainly had, but what came next was even more interesting and perhaps surprising. She was approached by former chief of staff of the Israel Defense Forces Lieutenant-General (Res.) Binyamin ("Benny") Gantz, who asked her to join him on the slate for his new political party, aptly named Israel Resilience. Gadeer initially refused. In fact, she refused three times before she agreed to join. While used to pushing the limits, she is also always careful to check and see if she is still working within acceptable communal boundaries. Although hesitant to put her name into the political ring, she ended up receiving a tremendous amount of support from the Druze community, an indication of how she had become a local celebrity and also how Druze society has progressed in their acceptance of women being active professionals outside the home. In politically turbulent times, the party did well, and Gadeer was swept into the Israeli parliament in 2019, becoming one of the youngest of the new members of Knesset at age thirty-four.

A Bridge to Positivity

When Gadeer talks about her place in the world, she states that she is a minority within a minority. She is an Israeli citizen, but she is not a Jew. She speaks Arabic, but she is not Muslim. As a consequence of this, she says proudly, "I can be a bridge – I can be the positive face of Israel not only in the region but also in the whole wide world." And indeed she can.

It might seem that Gadeer's life and surging career have been without setbacks. To the contrary. She experienced racism and sexism in the workplace. She acknowledges that when she started out as a television news reporter, she experienced a feeling of being different and an outsider. She is, however, at pains to stress that this has been the exception rather than the rule and prefers not to dwell on this part of her career. Gadeer overflows with positivity. She looks back without rancor and is determined to make a difference in her political career for her community, to ensure that the Druze people maintain a cherished position in Israeli society and that they are given everything they deserve.

In considering the sources of resilience in her life, she emphasizes that her family has always played a significant role in supporting her and helping her along her sometimes thorny path. In recent years, her community has as well come to her support, and if in earlier years this wasn't always the case, she now feels that they are firmly in her court. If we consider what else has helped her along her road, there is no question that a feeling of mission and purpose drives Gadeer and has helped shape who she is and how she approaches obstacles. She believes in what she is doing, wholeheartedly, and that sincerity is both very believable and very winning. The meaning that her hard work brings into her life is significant and plays an important role in her personal resilience, her ability to withstand the hardships of her career, including travel, long hours away from her children, and the stresses of politics.

She clearly also has ambition. With rising prominence, at only age thirty-six, she is setting her sights high and is definitely one to watch on the Israeli and international scene. Following the March 2020 election, Gadeer acted on her principles and decided not to enter the government coalition together with her leader Benny Gantz, instead joining the opposition with Yair Lapid's Yesh Atid Party (formerly allied with Gantz's Blue and White). The criticism she faced when choosing her career path, placing work outside the home as a value in addition to family and community, has dissipated. The rebukes she confronted are now just distant memories. Everybody wants to take credit for her success, but it is Gadeer Kamal Mreeh herself who has blazed her own trail, shattering the double-glazed glass ceiling to become Israel's first-ever female Druze MK.

CHAPTER 8

Lessons from the Sports Field

"We are on the map and we are here to stay."
Tal Brody, FIBA European Champions Cup, 1977

Path of Meaning

Imagine that you have to choose between two mutually exclusive paths. The first path is one that you have been toiling toward unceasingly for the last twelve years. It entails following a strict regimen of basketball practice and drill. This path is the fulfillment of your dreams. You have been chosen in the first round of the NBA draft to join the Baltimore Bullets and offered a salary in the millions of dollars. The second path is a year playing with a virtually unknown team in a small, war-torn country in the Middle East. This particular dilemma doesn't seem so difficult. It should be a no-brainer.

This was the choice that loomed on Tal Brody's horizon back in the summer of 1966, but as he tells the story, the choice for him was an easy one. And once he made his decision, Brody never looked back. Fifty years after coming to Israel, the 187-centimeter-tall (6 ft. 2 in.) Brody with his familiar smile is a celebrity in the Jewish state.

He reminisces on a life that began in Trenton, New Jersey, filled with achievements, awards, and recognition. This was a life replete with meaning and fulfillment, both personally and professionally. Sitting with the youthful-looking septuagenarian as he shares his life story, one cannot help but marvel at the honesty and straightforwardness that come shining through. More than any government leader, politician, diplomat, negotiator, or celebrity, it was basketball superstar Tal Brody who really and truly put Israel "on the map." Instantly recognizable among Israelis, Brody has become something of a national treasure.

Joining the Maccabi Tel Aviv team for one year, before planning to return to the United States to take up his offer with the Baltimore Bullets, Tal fell in love with Israel and stayed. Following that, only a short two-year hiatus interrupted more than fifty years of life in Israel. In 1968, Brody once again faced a dilemma of near-epic proportions. Receiving a draft notice from the US Army, he debated with himself whether to complete the aliyah immigration process he had begun in order to stay in Israel, or to return and serve his country of birth. Once again, according to Tal, he was faced with deciding between doing the "right" thing and doing what you really "want" to do. Choosing to answer the call, he returned to America and was drafted into the army for a two-year stint. After several grueling months training to be an infantry soldier, he was plucked out of his unit and certain deployment to Vietnam to join the Army basketball team, where he spent the remainder of his career with the armed forces playing ball and winning championships.

Upon completion of his US military service, Brody received a letter from Moshe Dayan, then defense minister of Israel, beseeching him to return to Maccabi Tel Aviv to raise the level of basketball in Israel. He was deeply touched by the letter and decided to come back to Israel, thus changing the trajectory of his life. Since then, Tal has spent half a century on and off the court, in business, as a family man with a wife and three children, and currently as a goodwill ambassador for Israel. In that capacity he represents the country overseas, often using basketball as a way to connect to people and share his love of his country.

Facing Great Odds

Dr. Fred Price, Brody's high school basketball coach, has remained his inspiration since Brody trained with him when he was in his teens. Price was not only a coach but also an exemplary educator, and the lessons that he taught young Tal have accompanied him for a lifetime. These are lessons Tal remembers and relates to even today, many decades after originally learning them:

- Look at the cup as half full.
- The people you meet going up the ladder are the same ones you will meet coming down.
- Expect difficulties. Consider them challenges.
- Don't sweat the small stuff. Keep your eye on the big picture.
- Persevere and you will win.

These are just some of the memorable phrases that run like a playlist in Tal's mind, looping continually and helping him through many a rough spot.

If anyone personifies perseverance in the face of great odds, it is Tal. The year was 1977. Israel had made it to the Euroleague Basketball Semi-Finals for the first time in history. The mood in Israel was somber, in the wake of the great losses incurred during the Yom Kippur War, less than four years earlier. A sense of the fragility of life was once again in the forefront of the Israeli psyche. On a fateful evening in April, all eyes were on the court in diplomatically neutral Virton, Belgium, where Maccabi Tel Aviv was meeting the Soviet Red Army team, CSKA, who had won four European Championships in as many years and had not lost a game for the past number of seasons. The odds were heavily against Maccabi. Yet aside from a few Soviet KGB agents, the enthusiastic crowd consisted of hundreds of Israeli supporters. The blue and white flag dominated the arena, and the language heard courtside was Hebrew. The stadium collectively held its breath as the final basket sunk through the net propelled by Captain Tal Brody, bringing in victory at the final buzzer with an upset win of 91 to 79.

In the seconds after the surprising turnaround, a reporter caught sight of the jubilant Brody and stuck a microphone under his nose. Brody's response, broadcast on live TV to a euphoric nation, was to become iconic: "We are on the map, and we are here to stay." In those few short words, Tal Brody encapsulated the sentiments of the Maccabi fans and underscored the tenaciousness and perseverance of the entire nation. The phrase has since taken on a life of its own, becoming emblematic of a generation of Israelis and symbolizing a confidence that their little country, always punching above its weight but hitherto existentially endangered, was here to stay.

The High Road

Choosing between the moral imperative and the temptations of ego and fame, Tal has always chosen the high road and counsels young people he meets both in the sport arena and in daily life to do the same. Aside from that momentous decision to come to Israel and leave fame and fortune behind, he was faced with a moral dilemma one week before the European Cup Finals, in 1977, as the team was getting ready to fly to Belgrade. Tal received word that his father had suffered a heart attack and was in the intensive care unit. Without wavering or hesitating, he made his way to the airport and flew off to the United States, not knowing whether he would eventually make it to the finals, but knowing that he was doing the right thing. He found his father recuperating, and at his urging, Tal made a quick U-turn and returned to

John F. Kennedy Airport only to discover that the ticket arranged for by his team had not arrived at the Yugoslav ticketing desk at the airport. Demanding to see the person in charge, Brody found himself facing a startled Yugoslav ticket officer who remembered Brody from a game he had played in Ljubljana the previous season. The official allowed Tal to board the plane without a ticket. For Tal this was a vindication that he had indeed done the right thing and was thus being rewarded. He arrived in Belgrade just in time for the final game.

Exploring the resilient fiber that runs through Tal Brody, one clearly can see that meaning and meaning-making are critical features of resilience. Victor Frankl characterized this best when he talked about how a person can withstand the most difficult trials if he has a purpose in life. Frankl was, of course, referencing his experiences as a concentration camp inmate during the Holocaust, where he witnessed people on both sides of the divide. There were those who gave up and perished, and others who hung on tenaciously with the fire of purpose burning in their hearts and minds. Even in situations that are not life and death, finding meaning contributes to feeling one's life has been well lived and to having the ability to meet day-to-day challenges and overcome obstacles.

Tal Brody exemplifies this kind of meaning when he talks about how meaningful it was for him playing for the Israeli team. According to Brody, the Israeli basketball team has had a huge impact on the Jewish communities wherever they have played, whether it be in Los Angeles, Paris, or Peru. The sense that the "shtetl Jew" has shed his shadow and can now stand tall and win on the professional basketball court has been a source of great pride to Tal, and he feels the generations of Jews cheering on the sidelines.

Life can be full of ups and downs, and Tal's life has been no exception. While he is reticent to delve into the rough times he encountered, he is eager to share the keys to his personal resilience. For example, what helped him make that fateful decision to leave the NBA, without second-guessing himself and wondering whether he was doing the right thing? What helped him adapt to his new country, language, and culture? What helped him weather the vagaries of business? Brody cites three key factors: a basic optimism, an ability to keep perspective and focus on the larger picture, and flexibility. Humor, he adds, doesn't hurt either. When asked about Israeli resilience from a national perspective, he unhesitatingly points to the ability of Israelis to come together in a crisis to open their hearts and their homes for strangers and to give freely of themselves. This is a perfect example of the concept of social support and how it is critical for the building and maintenance of resilience.

For Tal Brody, resilience is a way of life. It is something you work at, something you practice, and something you do. Resilience doesn't happen automatically or all by itself. Setting goals and then developing a steady practice are things Tal understands very well, and he does practice what he preaches. It is that outlook and perspective that gave him the confidence to make the right decisions on his path in life. The confidence, indeed, to declare just eighteen years after its reestablishment that a small Middle-Eastern country was now well and truly "on the map."

CHAPTER 9

Determination and Discovery

"Don't blame others. It all depends on you!"
Dr. Amit Goffer

Hitting the Brakes

When Dr. Amit Goffer's wife bought him a new pair of pants at the local mall, the last thing he expected to receive along with the clothes was a winning raffle ticket. The prize was a new quad bike, colloquially known as a *tractaron*. It was a win as surprising as it was unwanted. Goffer simply had no use for an all-terrain vehicle (ATV), and he decided not to redeem the prize.

His children were less than pleased with this decision. In an effort to make it up to them, Dr. Goffer, a successful CEO of a magnetic resonance imaging (MRI) company, took them out for a day of riding on ATVs. If they couldn't own one, at least they could rent a couple of them for the day and enjoy the ride. His son was in one vehicle, and Amit rode behind him together with his daughter on a second ATV. Approaching a steep downward slope, Goffer hit the brakes, and his vehicle bumped into something, causing him to fly through the branches of a tree at literally breakneck speed before crashing to the ground. On impact he could feel nothing. He could not move his arms or legs and immediately knew that he had broken his neck. In an instant, he had become a quadriplegic.

Nearly twenty years later, we are sitting in the living room of his modern, suburban home near the Jezreel Valley in the north of Israel. Sunshine is peeking out of gray skies after the season's first rains. Toys are scattered around the room, a reminder of Dr. Goffer's grandchildren who regularly visit. His desk is covered with papers attesting to the multiple projects he is involved with. Seated in his wheelchair using a specially customized mouse, Goffer logs on to a CNN breaking news item showcasing the innovation of his latest company.

Amit Goffer has been to hell and back, but, in doing so, he has changed the lives of paraplegics around the world. His current success is the result not only of his intelligence and ingenuity but also of his resolve and resilience at a pivotal moment of his recovery from this life-altering accident. Turning a tragedy that could easily have led to a downward spiral into a challenge to be met, Goffer chose to be spurred forward by his accident rather than set back. As a result, his innovations have transformed the world of paraplegics.

At Eye Level

Long before his life-changing injury, Amit Goffer was an outstanding student who excelled in innovation. While service in the Israel Defense Forces is mandatory, a few exceptional students are selected for a special track that includes academic studies prior to their service. Goffer was just such a student. After graduating from the Technion–Israel Institute of Technology in electrical engineering, Amit served for five years in the IDF, becoming a captain in the Israeli Air Force. The Israeli army was, in his words, "a unique University of Life. You go through a process in the army which is very positive, and it has an impact on the rest of your life – the people, the sense of contribution, and the fact that you are working for your country." During his army stint, he was in charge of several defense projects, most of them too secret to discuss till this day, so many years later. The amount of responsibility given to him at a young age taught him how to think out of the box. That is only one of the many contributions he ascribes to his army experience. He underscores the contribution of army service to his own personal development as well as that of so many Israeli youngsters.

Goffer served in the IDF after the Yom Kippur War of October 1973. He and his peers experienced the stark contrast between the lightning Israeli defeat of its enemies in only six days back in 1967 and the great losses suffered by Israel after a surprise simultaneous attack by Syria and Egypt on Yom Kippur, the holiest day of the year. At one point, while working on secret experiments at an isolated IDF base, Goffer complained to his superior, Yair Shamir, the son of former prime minister Yitzchak Shamir, raising his voice as he listed what was wrong with his equipment and issuing a list of demands needed for his research. Instead of dismissing the rantings of his subordinate or punishing him for behavior that was unacceptable, Shamir listened patiently and then made sure that Goffer received everything that he needed.

Having a supportive community around you helps build resilience, and Goffer cites the environment that was created in his unit by his commanding officer. "He cared about the mission, above all. The fact that someone more junior than him was yelling at a commanding officer was not important. Ours is a different kind of army." Goffer compares the IDF to other military organizations, highlighting the ability to question authority – not taking anything as a given – and the critical and analytical thinking that is characteristic of Israelis. Goffer summarizes, "We have a different kind of approach."

Following his army service, Goffer, by then married with three children, began working at Raphael Defense Systems. Subsequently he began his postdoctoral work at Drexel University in Philadelphia. While at Drexel, he had two advisors, one American and the other Israeli. Goffer learned from both of his advisors, albeit in different ways. While working with his older American advisor, Goffer was acutely aware of the "pecking order." In contrast, his Israeli advisor encouraged him to feel confident about his abilities and urged Goffer to see him and other professors and professionals *"b'govah einayim,"* a Hebrew expression that means "at eye level." Understanding the importance of not being intimidated by higher-ups or letting them restrain his creativity would become critical to Amit's future endeavors.

The Only Way Up

Reflecting on the immediate days, weeks, and months following his accident, Amit acknowledges he felt that he had fallen into a deep chasm. "The way I saw it then," he says, "I was in a very deep hole… I was in deep depression. I wished I hadn't survived the accident. So many people don't survive such accidents, and I wondered why I did." Goffer had overcome medical challenges in the past, having fully recovered from life-threatening leukemia a decade earlier. Now he would need to dig his way out of an even harsher circumstance.

Drawing on his own inner resilience, he came to the conclusion that "I knew I couldn't fall any deeper. The only way was up. I had to climb out of the hole toward the light." In Greek mythology, while overcome by his grief, Orpheus ventures to the Underworld to bring his beloved Eurydice back to life. Amit references Orpheus when crediting his wife as being the one to bring him back from his personal abyss. His children also motivated him to recover: "I refused to give up the role of being a father." The tremendous support of his family and the meaning and purpose derived from his important role in his family's life helped him climb out of the depths.

The support and goodwill of friends added another layer of community that helped his ascent toward the light. Goffer remembers one particular friend, Aaron, who encouraged him to leave the house for the first time. "Although my friends' positive reactions felt like a hug, my thoughts were not directed at them but were focused on myself. When you go outside, you carry much emotional baggage with you. You worry about things, such as *will I embarrass myself?*" Getting to Aaron's house required navigating a dirt road. Aaron had engaged a tractor to smooth out the road so that Amit could get to his house by wheelchair. When heavy rains fell and the road flooded, Aaron once again used a tractor to restore its accessibility for his friend. This gesture touched Goffer deeply, and he recalls it to this day with a smile, even though it happened so many years ago.

After reaching a plateau in his physical rehabilitation, confined to a wheelchair but with his depression lifting, Goffer began to ponder why the sole solution for paralyzed people was the wheelchair. It had been created in the 1700s, and since then virtually no progress had been made in helping paraplegics move around. There must be, he thought, a way to help paraplegics walk again. His innovative, entrepreneurial mind began to whir, its personal, professional, and business sides coming together synergistically in his search for a solution. As former Israeli president Shimon Peres commented: "When you have two alternatives, the first thing you have to do is to look for the third that you didn't think about, that doesn't exist." A wearable robotic exoskeleton that would literally put disabled people back on their feet was the innovative idea Amit came up with. The desire to bring his vision to life combined with the need to return to his previous functioning kept him going. Reflecting on this invention, Goffer notes that the injury brought something superhuman out of him.

With the help of government and private funding, he was able to create the exoskeleton. Clinical trials were held at Tel Hashomer Hospital, where Goffer himself had undergone rehabilitation. ReWalk,

Goffer's product, has helped many paraplegics get back on their feet. Ironically, due to the extent of his injuries, Dr. Goffer himself cannot use the ReWalk exoskeleton and is still confined to a wheelchair. When asked how he feels seeing people walk again using his invention, Amit points to a photo of himself on the day in New York when ReWalk filed for an initial public offering (IPO) on Nasdaq to raise $58 million at a company value of $250–300 million. The inventor is pictured sitting in his wheelchair, surrounded by several "ReWalkers" who are all standing upright thanks to Goffer's robotic exoskeleton. They have their hands placed symbolically on Amit's torso in a gesture honoring the man who has given their mobility back to them. "Entrepreneurs talk about the thrill of an exit. I love money as much as anyone else, but what I have received from the ReWalkers and their families is something that no exit can compete with."

Choosing to Smile

Is ingenuity inherent in Israeli society? Goffer believes it is, and feels that he himself personifies this trait that is a product of ancient Judaism and modern chutzpah. Having been taught that each Israeli soldier has "the baton of the chief of staff in his bag," meaning that anyone can assume greatness, Goffer contends that this education begins young. Appreciation for nonconformity and creativity are also part of the Israeli educational process. In contrast, he recalls that when he and his family lived in America, the parents were invited to school around Thanksgiving and saw pictures of turkeys that the kids had painted. All of the turkeys were brown except for one, which was all the colors of the rainbow. The name on that painting was Yuval Goffer, Amit's son, a demonstration of Israeli individuality that made his father proud.

In analyzing Dr. Goffer's resilience, several factors come into play. Without a doubt, support from family and friends was key in his recovery. Without them, he would not have made it back from the abyss. They are in fact what brought him back to life, but what helped him thrive? In looking back, his advice to anyone grappling with the aftermath of an accident, illness, or major setback is not to assign blame, whether it is to doctors, others involved, or anyone else. He advises getting help; remembering that even though you're suffering, the people around you are suffering too; seeing the glass as half full; and setting a goal. Remind yourself that you are in charge – the path you choose is in your hands, and, as he says, "it is up to you whether you have a smile or a frown. So smile." His native intelligence, skill, and ability to think out of the box provided him with the tools to continue to create. This creative urge has powered the drive he has discovered to make the lives of paraplegics better. His life has meaning. His creativity has a purpose. His resilience thrives.

Amit recalls receiving acclaim after being the keynote speaker at a conference in London, only to attend a reception afterwards where the cocktail tables were out of reach and the guest of honor sat in his wheelchair at "ass-level" while other guests shifted awkwardly around him. "Being a grown-up at the height of a child is a humiliating experience. There is a loss of dignity and self-esteem." Despite the fact that ReWalk was not helpful to him personally, Goffer would not give up and continued his work to help himself and others stand upright again. His most recent invention – the UpNRide – resembles a specially customized scooter, a two-wheeled robotic device with supports to help paralyzed users get up and moving. This time Goffer was able to benefit. With UpNRide, Goffer was moving upright and outdoors, after two decades of being confined to a wheelchair. In 2015, Goffer unveiled UpNRide at the huge Rehacare Trade Fair in Dusseldorf, Germany. Following his presentation, Dr. Amit Goffer enjoyed lunch with his colleagues and hosts, this time eating at tall reception tables. Amit's invention, pioneered in the aftermath of tragedy, had restored him back to "eye level."

CHAPTER 10

Against the Stream

"When you believe in your cause, nothing can stop you."

Yoseph Haddad

In the Spotlight

The studio lights were bearing down on the guests at Newzroom Afrika, the twenty-four-hour news channel based in Johannesburg, South Africa. Four guests sat opposite the host, Lindi Sirame, as Muhammed Desai, cofounder of BDS South Africa, the local branch of the anti-Israel Boycott, Divestment, and Sanctions campaign, turned the conversation to the ongoing COVID-19 pandemic. "In Israel, you have the Israeli Ministry of Health that issues notices to its population, which includes Palestinians, but they only issue them in Hebrew, not in Arabic." Immediately a strident voice countered, "That is a lie. Stop the lying." The person behind that voice knew of what he spoke. "I live in Israel," he said. "Moreover, I think the audience should know who I am. I am an Israeli Arab, and I received the coronavirus instructions in Arabic. So, number one, stop lying. And number two, ask me – I will tell you the truth."

Yoseph, spelled in phonetic English as it would be in Hebrew but pronounced the Arabic way ("Youseff"), is a sharply good-looking and youthful man, polished and determined to take the offensive. Not allowing false accusations about his country to go unchallenged, he regularly writes and broadcasts in Hebrew, English, and Arabic, with many of his social media posts going viral. The bravery and sincerity of this young Israeli Arab is met with a warm embrace by people of goodwill across Israel and around the world. However, not everyone is happy with Yoseph, and his outspoken activism is not without risk. Yoseph is constantly attacked for his views and has even received death threats from extremists.

Dueling Perspectives

Arab citizens of Israel make up just over 20 percent of the country's population. Among them there is a diversity of opinions, just as in any community. The majority define themselves as Arab Israelis, some consider their identity just Arab, some call themselves Palestinian. Around three-quarters of Israel's Arab citizens are Sunni Muslims, with the remainder being Bedouins, Christian Arabs, Druze, and Circassian. Druze Arabic-speakers live distinctly from the larger Arab populations, as do the Circassian community. Whereas America is often described as a melting pot, Israel sees itself more as a mosaic: the different parts do not always overlap, but they do form together to create a greater whole.

Polls show that a majority of Arab citizens of Israel are proud of their nationality, but the situation is complex indeed. The voice heard in the media and the picture painted in public is largely represented by the Arab parties in the Knesset, which tend to verge toward more extreme positions. In fact, they are often at odds with their electorate, many of whom would like them to join a government and wield political influence, something that has not happened yet in the modern State of Israel. While Arab citizens tend to agree that life in Israel is good and comparatively much better than in other Middle Eastern countries, some have difficulty grappling with the reality of being a minority in a Jewish country. Parts of the community support Palestinian nationalistic goals, which call for the destruction and dismantling of the State of Israel, although this is a minority view. While considered by some a potential fifth column during the first decade of Israel's existence, Israeli Arabs have made giant steps forward integrating into all the professions and businesses. The quest for equality, as in any country but especially sensitive with Middle Eastern geopolitics at play in the background, is something that society continues to grapple with.

Yoseph's activism is not always well received in his community. There are those who think that that he goes too far and that he should be ostracized for going against the stream. This does not seem to bother this outspoken man and certainly does not slow him down. Where does Yoseph come from, and how did he come to this unusual place where only a small number of Israeli Arabs have publicly dared to tread?

Yoseph grew up in Nazareth, the largest city in northern Israel and a predominantly Arab town, comprised of both Muslims and Christians. The second of four children, Yoseph has two sisters and one brother. His parents taught their children to be open-minded, to explore and question the world around them but, above all, to be good people, contributing to the world. Yoseph recalls that his parents strongly encouraged the children to integrate into Israeli society. Yoseph's perfect English and unaccented Hebrew is such because while Arabic was spoken in the family home for five days each week, the remaining two days were split with one day only Hebrew spoken and the other day, only English. If the children did not approach their parents in the language of the day, they would not receive an answer! This interesting arrangement resulted in trilingual offspring, with everyone being fluent in each of Israel's three main languages Arabic, Hebrew, and English.

Yoseph was born in Haifa, and the family moved to Nazareth when he was a youngster. Most of his extended family and friends lived in Haifa, populated by a mix of Jews, Muslims, Christians and others, so as a youngster, Yoseph would often take the bus to Haifa to play soccer with children from all different backgrounds. After completing high school, Yoseph, like most eighteen-year-olds, was faced with big decisions about his future. Jewish Israelis are subject to a universal draft into the Israel Defense Forces. Arabs and Bedouins are exempt from this mandatory service due to the sensitivities of both their communities and the realities of Israeli army service. However, they can volunteer to serve if they so wish. Only a few take that route, but Yoseph, who has never taken the easy way out, decided to volunteer for IDF service in a combat unit. And if he had any shred of doubt about serving in Israel's army, a horrific act was about to affirm why taking that step was the right thing to do.

Coexistence under Attack

The Maxim restaurant in Haifa is more than just an eatery. Jointly owned by Arab and Jewish proprietors, and overlooking the sea, it is a symbol of the city and its ethos of tolerance and coexistence. On October 4, 2003, that very symbolism made it a target. Two days before Yom Kippur, a twenty-eight-year-old woman entered the restaurant, which was bustling with people. A law student – on the verge of qualifying as an attorney – from Jenin (a city in the Palestinian Authority, not far from Haifa), she had been recruited by Palestinian Islamic Jihad terrorists. She detonated the powerful bomb belt that she was wearing, and the results of the attack were devastating. Twenty-one innocent people were murdered, and over sixty people were injured. Reports from first-responders at the scene told of a macabre aftermath. The casualties mirrored the diversity of the clientele. Five members of a single Jewish family – the Zer-Avivs – were killed in the attack. The

Arab head waiter, Hana Francis; waiter Sharbal Matar, twenty-three; and cook Osama Najar, twenty-eight, were killed. Another five members of one family – the Almogs – also died. Ten-year-old Oran Almog survived, but in addition to losing two of his grandparents, his father, his brother, and his cousin, he also lost his sight in the blast.

The Maxim restaurant bombing took place just as Yoseph Haddad was about to begin his IDF service. The response to Yoseph's decision to enlist in the IDF was mixed. It simply was not a usual decision to take for someone from his community. Some of his friends were so upset with his decision that they ended their friendship with him immediately. A handful of them have never spoken to him again. Yet others supported him, although this was a step that they themselves would never take. Years later, many of Yoseph's friends have shared with him in confidence that they wished they had followed his example, and if they could do it over again, they too would have enlisted. This underlies Yoseph's contention that he in fact represents the unspoken majority of the Arab Israeli community, not the minority view, as the media would have you believe. Yoseph's parents were most supportive of his decision, although his mother was understandably worried about his safety. The Maxim attack affirmed to Yoseph what he had already decided, that serving in defense of his people – Arab and Jewish – and his country was what he needed to do.

Overcoming Injury

Yoseph's army service took him to the frontline of the fight against terrorism. He drafted into the Golani infantry brigade. His comrades, hailing from a variety of places and backgrounds, welcomed him with open arms. He went on to become a commander in the brigade and served on Israel's borders in the north and south of the country. Throughout his IDF service, Yoseph had no doubts about the rectitude of what he was doing. Even as he found himself, an Arab, fighting for the Jewish state inside the Arab country of Lebanon during the 2006 Second Lebanon War, he felt certain about his role.

The summer of 2006 was very hot indeed. The enemy was not Lebanon or the Lebanese people, but rather the terrorists of Hezbollah. They had been responsible for launching volley after volley of rocket and missile attacks on communities in northern Israel during that conflict, which injured over 1,350 civilians and killed 44. Yoseph's brigade was among those tasked with finding IDF soldiers who had been kidnapped and taking out Hezbollah's rocket-launching capability. Nearly half of those killed by Hezbollah rockets were Arab citizens of Israel, including two babies from Yoseph's hometown, Nazareth. For him, this war was personal.

One of the fiercest battles of the war took place in Bint Jbeil, a large town in southern Lebanon with a population of around twenty thousand. Hezbollah had turned it into a stronghold, embedding their fighters among families, homes, and businesses to create a human shield around them. As a combat soldier in the city, Yoseph recalls being approached by a Lebanese man who entreated him in Arabic, "We welcome you. Please, please, beat Hezbollah." The irony of a Lebanese Arab making this plea to an Israeli Arab soldier was not lost on Yoseph. During the conflict, he lost many friends in battle, as well as his deputy commander, Major Roi Klein, who heroically jumped on a grenade to save the lives of his soldiers.

As the war was winding down, just two days before a cease-fire was declared, Hezbollah fired an anti-tank missile toward the position that Yoseph and his fellow soldiers were defending. The missile hit a wall close to Yoseph, causing him to be thrown several meters. His first thought was, "What will I tell my mother?" He knew immediately that he had been badly injured. His mom would indeed have cause to worry: Yoseph's foot had been severed. He was evacuated to a helicopter by his comrades, still under fire, and taken to the Galilee Medical

Center in Nahariya. Several surgeries later, Yoseph woke and raised his head to discover his foot had been successfully reattached.

Grueling months of recovery and rehabilitation ensued. Yoseph kept his focus on his goal of resuming the active life he had prior to his injury and was able to maintain his high spirits, even when the medical prognosis he received was disappointing. He was told he was lucky to have his foot back, and while his doctor thought he would walk again, they expected that he would limp. Yoseph turned to the doctor and said, "You watch! I will play soccer again!" Competitive and determined, Yoseph set about trying to prove the doctors wrong. He worked hard at rehabilitation, advancing more quickly than expected. One year after the injury, Yoseph went for his final checkup. He entered the doctor's office with a soccer ball, with which he then proceeded to demonstrate his considerable soccer skills right there in the office. He had achieved his goal. Not only does he walk without a limp, nowadays, Yoseph runs ten kilometers (six miles) every week.

Creating an Outlet

Following his military service, Yoseph moved to Canada, where he worked for a couple of years before returning to Israel as COO of a marketing research company based in Tel Aviv. It was a well-paid job with great benefits, including something prized by working Tel Avivians in Israel's busy urban business center: a parking space. After five years, he decided to give this all up and establish a nonprofit organization. He quit his job and cofounded Together We Vouch for Each Other, which has a board comprised of Christian, Jewish, Muslim, and Druze Israelis. The focus of his organization is to encourage full Arab integration and participation in Israeli society, all the while being a vocal opponent to misinformation about his country. All this has given his life a sense of purpose that working in business could not. As the organization grows, more people from diverse backgrounds are joining the movement. It is hard not to be won over by Yoseph's charisma and dynamism, but most of all, his conviction and passion for the cause. He is confident that he and his organization best represent the Arab consensus within Israel.

A self-appointed ambassador for Israel, Yoseph has no problem talking about societal problems and where Israel needs to improve. Israel is not perfect, he contends, but no country is, and dialogue is healthy. He states that he is not there just to criticize, but rather to help be part of the solution to problems that trouble him as a citizen. His organization is committed to playing its part in the Jewish and democratic state of Israel within which its members are proud to live. He sees his role as demolishing the narrative of extremists on both sides of the spectrum. To extremist Jews who claim Arabs do not want to be part of the Jewish state, he serves as an example of an Arab who served his country in uniform. To the Arab extremists, he is showing that the majority of Jews want Arab citizens to be equal and to share a positive role in society. "If both extremes are against us, I must be on the right path," he says with a smile and a twinkle in his eye.

"Until recently," he says, "most Israeli Arabs who thought like me didn't dare speak out. What our organization has done is to say to those people: Don't be afraid. We've got your back. Together we can make a change." The response has been immense. He and his cause have garnered tens of thousands of followers on social media. While some of the public responses to him are fiercely critical, the private messages are generally supportive. It is hard for the Arab community to praise Yoseph's message. Even his sister, Yoseph says, is careful about how encouraging she can be to his posts, publicly. Each time she sees his work on social media, she begins typing, "Brother, I am so proud of you," but before her comment has been fully typed, she often deletes it for fear that extremists may curse and threaten her. This is something that Yoseph fully understands. "When I speak one on one with someone from the Arab community, they often say, 'Keep doing what you're doing.' But if that same person is with other Arabs, he changes the way he talks. Even in a group where most people think the same thing, they're afraid to say it out loud."

Yoseph has embarked on extensive speaking tours around the world, talking with groups of students on campuses abroad as well as groups of students visiting Israel, presenting a side of Israel that few are familiar with. He shares the experience of growing up in the Arab community of Israel, living alongside Jews. Many university campuses have long been hotbeds for anti-Israel activism, led by radical, often antisemitic groups. Yoseph's voice is credible, as evidenced by a speaking engagement that he took part in at Harvard University. Yoseph asked the moderator not to introduce him in any way before he began his presentation. Twenty-five minutes into it, a student from the political science department derided Israel, saying critically: "This is the exact type of presentation I would expect from an Israeli Jew." With his most Arabic-sounding accent, Yoseph replied: "Actually, my name is Youseff Haddad, and I am an Arab Israeli." The questioner was stunned. It was unimaginable to him that the passion for Israel given voice to came from not only an Israeli citizen, but an Arab one at that. This is why, contends Yoseph, his engagement with the public is so important.

Yoseph Haddad is well aware of the complexities and the disputes that populate his world, but he is fiercely proud to be an Israeli. There has been a lot of discussion in the media about "Hatikvah," Israel's national anthem, and how it is problematic for the non-Jewish citizens of Israel, beginning, as it does, with the words, "As long as in the heart within, the Jewish soul yearns…" When asked about this, Yoseph answers immediately. "Do I have a problem with the 'Hatikvah'? Yes. Do I sing the 'Hatikvah'? Yes. Do I change one word in the 'Hatikvah'? Yes." He has no wish for the country to change the words, it is just something that he does for himself. Instead of saying "Jewish soul," he changes it to "Israeli soul."

He illustrates this with a story. He was once at a ceremony for wounded IDF veterans in Canada. Prior to addressing the audience, Yoseph and three Jewish veterans were on stage as first the Canadian national anthem and then the Israeli national anthem were sung. One of the IDF vets turned to him and asked him if he would sing the Israeli anthem. He replied in the affirmative and noted that he would just change that one word from Jewish to Israeli. They went onstage and the ceremony began. Following a rendition of "Oh, Canada," Joseph began to sing the "Hatikvah" along with the other vets. When he got to the word he was about to change, he heard all three of his Jewish comrades do exactly the same thing alongside him, and a tear came to his eyes. When their presentation was finished and they exited the stage, Yoseph had the chance to ask them why they too changed the word, and the others replied, "We are brothers. We couldn't let you sing alone."

Finding Your Voice

Yoseph is someone who clearly chooses to swim against the stream and is willing to fight uphill battles for things he passionately believes in, even if his beliefs are unpopular with many and often garner responses that would scare a more timid individual. What gives Yoseph this strength to speak out loudly and clearly for his beliefs? What helped him bounce back from his injury? What is the secret to Yoseph's personal resilience?

A dose of good old Israeli chutzpah as one of the keys to his own resilience. He speaks his mind, is articulate, and is not willing to step down. This is a quintessential Israeli characteristic that he seems to have an adequate measure of. He is impatient. This too is an aspect of chutzpah. He wants things to happen now and is not willing to wait.

He will go out and fight for what he wants and not worry about the consequences. On deeper reflection about the characteristics of resilience that underlie Yoseph's life choices and actions, the importance of community and meaning are ever present. The encouragement he has received for standing up and speaking out has strengthened him through the more difficult moments that he has encountered. Surrounding oneself with a supportive, sympathetic, and encouraging environment is an important aspect in building personal resilience.

Aside from finding community and support, an additional feature of Yoseph's resilience is the meaning with which his life is imbued. Yoseph has often chosen to forge his own unique, nonconformist path for things that he very much believes in. This belief gives him strength and propels him to stand up and brave the storm that he often attracts like a lightning rod. Thus, community and meaning seem to be key in Yoseph's life at this juncture. He is young, and the future is promising. It will be interesting to keep an eye on this maverick as he makes his way in the world. And what makes him brave enough to persistently go against the stream? "If a Hezbollah rocket didn't stop me, nothing will."

CHAPTER 11

Loss and Life

"Resilience is about becoming, not overcoming."

Sherri Mandell

The Unimaginable

The day dawned bright and clear on May 8, 2001, with no hint of the life-shattering tragedy that would rip apart Sherri Mandell's well-ordered life and family just a few hours later. Her eldest son Koby, five weeks short of his fourteenth birthday, had decided to play hooky from school and went off with a classmate for a hike in the nearby wadi, a canyon that was a mere ten-minute walk from his house. The trail winding through the wadi is literally in the backyard of Tekoa, a small village located south of Jerusalem and east of Hebron that the Mandells call home. It is a beautiful expanse of Judean desert scenery. This canyon has it all: earth tones, jagged rocks, cliffs, and caves that were inhabited by monks in the second and third century CE seeking solitude and a place to connect to God. It is a favorite place for hiking and communing with nature. It is a quiet, peaceful place, where people go to escape the pressures of everyday life, to find silence and solace. That sunny morning in May, however, the canyon turned into a place of horror.

Koby and his friend, Yosef Ishran, were brutally murdered by Palestinian terrorists: first kidnapped and bound, the boys were then stabbed and stoned to death. A local sheep rancher graphically described how the terrorists left the boys' mutilated bodies to be found by the search parties who went out looking when the hour got late and the boys had not returned home.

Sherri, an articulate and lively fifty-something, greets us in her house in the village of Tekoa with a ready smile and an easy laugh. It is the better part of two decades since that fateful day, and Koby would have been in his early thirties by now. Sherri easily recalls the horrors of the first few days and weeks after Koby's death; the memories of the aftermath of his murder are still palpable. She vividly recalls a searing pain so sharp that she thought she was going to die. She *wanted* to die. She also remembers the words that picked her up and propelled her forward. Her husband Seth, a rabbi and educator, said to her, "We have three children who need us. We will not ruin their lives." Those words, along with the togetherness that they were able to find amidst the grief both within the family and their community, allowed them to rise and not only return to the living, but to go on and create the Koby Mandell Foundation, an organization that helps bereaved families and has created therapeutic healing programs for thousands of children and adults. Taking their personal tragedy and turning their grief into an organization that provides services for a hitherto overlooked element in society has given meaning and purpose to Sherri's life and helped her deal with the death of her beloved eldest son.

Journey of Healing

Returning to those early days and months after the murder, the daily visits from her good friend Shira, who also happened to be a grief counselor, were perhaps the most important part of her healing. Shira not only massaged her weekly, but reassured her that it was okay to cry and mourn, comparing her situation to that of a baby who would need to relearn how to walk. When Sherri was ready to come out of her cocoon of grief and to begin walking, Shira was right by her side to walk with her. Along with the daily visits from her friend, the feeling of solidarity, of being one with her husband, Seth, further supported her during this dark time. According to Sherri, she and Seth have very different personalities and different ways of being in the world. Yet after Koby's death, she felt that they were together, in her words, "one body with two heads." This feeling gave her the strength to carry on.

Shira not only visited on a daily basis, she also guided Sherri in her responses to her grieving children and to life events. When grappling with how to deal with the constant flow of tears, Sherri tried Shira's suggestion that she give the kids a clock and tell them to time her, stopping her after one minute. The kids, then aged twelve, eleven, and six, readily agreed and became the timekeepers for their mom's tears. This unique intervention allowed Sherri to cry when she needed to, yet provided a boundary both for herself and for her kids, who soon realized that Mom would cry, and then Mom would stop.

Another suggestion of Shira's became a very powerful mechanism for the family to remember Koby in an active and meaningful way. As his fourteenth birthday neared, a mere five weeks after the murder, Shira encouraged Sherri and Seth to commemorate the day by doing something special. The family decided to give alms to fourteen beggars in Jerusalem, as giving charity was something that Koby loved to do. The situation became almost comical, as they had trouble finding enough needy people to distribute money to. They had to actually chase some of them down, leading to slapstick scenes filled with healing laughter. The family continued this tradition for many years, each year adding another person in need to equal the number of years Koby would have been. As they neared Koby's thirtieth birthday, they wondered whether they would find the requisite thirty beggars, or perhaps it was indeed time to lay this custom to rest.

Laughter has been a constant theme of healing in the Mandell house. Both Seth and Sherri are naturally funny and laugh a lot, and Koby was a funny kid himself who always loved a good laugh. The theme of laughter has become one of the ways the Koby Foundation has supported its activities, creating evenings of laughter called Comedy with Koby. These evenings bring laughter and good times to the world and have helped the foundation reach its annual fundraising goals.

Looking back over the years since Koby's death, Sherri shares that the infusion of spirituality into her life has been one of the great surprises. By her own admission, she had never been a very spiritual person, not interested in past lives, reincarnation, or the life of the soul. However, after Koby's death, she was literally "hit on the head" with it, in the form of birds that kept bumping into her, dying on her doorstep, flying into her house and car, all of them as if coming with a message from Koby saying, "I am here." This element of spirituality has found a warm place in Sherri's heart, as she went on to study pastoral counseling, continue with Torah study, and combine both of these in the writing of two books: *The Blessing of a Broken Heart* and *The Road to Resilience: From Chaos to Celebration*.

When considering her own resilience, Sherri says that she is not resilient by nature. At the time of Koby's death, she felt fragile and on the brink of either insanity or death. Yet with the support of family, friends, and community, and by identifying a spiritual link to Koby, she returned to life. Since that time, she has found ways to reach out to others dealing with the death of a loved one, to provide support, advice, and a shining example of how to continue.

Grief and Gratitude

The culture of bereavement in Israel is pervasive. The term "family of grief" is an inclusive one. Anyone who has lost a family member in war, during army service, or in a terror attack "joins" this family and is embraced by them. There is public acknowledgement of this grief and loss on both the national and community levels. This manifests itself most prominently when public ceremonies occur on Israel's Memorial Day, commemorated one day before Israel's Independence Day. The juxtaposition of these two days, while perhaps jarring, underscores how Israelis honor the sacrifices that have been made to ensure its sometimes tenuous existence. Families of the bereaved are invited to special ceremonies and visited by dignitaries, including the top brass of the military and national leaders. Parents and siblings are interviewed on radio and television, and there is government support to help the families memorialize their loved ones in a variety of ways, ranging from books published in the deceased's memory to a hiking trail carved out of the wilderness and named for the deceased.

Transitioning from the depths of sadness brought on by Memorial Day to the excitement and pure joy of celebrating the actual creation and existence of the modern State of Israel can be challenging. How does one move from grief to joy instantaneously? The radio in Israel mirrors that difficult transition. During Memorial Day, sad songs are played all day long. In the late afternoon, as the sun begins its descent, the music begins to change its beat, and minor key subtly changes to major. By the eve of Independence Day, it is full-out merriment and joy. Honoring those who have sacrificed their lives, acknowledging the tremendous sacrifice and sharing the grief of the families leads the way into thanksgiving for the country we have. This is the core of Israeli resilience.

In Israel, children meet death at a much earlier age than in other countries of the West. It is not unusual to see a child attending a funeral in Israel, and schools hold memorial services for the victims of the Holocaust as well as for soldiers and terror victims. Indeed, even the youngest of children are exposed to these losses when the special sirens sound and the entire country stands still for a moment of silence in honor of the fallen. This embrace of bereaved victims of terror and soldiers who have found death on the battlefield or in training is at the very core of Israeli society. It impacts the way that Israelis deal with civilian deaths as well. Funerals are generally large and well attended. Visiting the bereaved is part of the fabric of life: yearly memorial services are held to commemorate grandparents or parents who are long gone. Death is very much a part of life in Israel.

The presence of death in Israel introduces one more face in the mosaic that has created Israeli resilience. By necessity, death is present, and because Israelis tend to be straightforward, it is not skirted around. Learning how to live life to the fullest while not forgetting about the deceased is at the heart of a resilient approach. It involves understanding that there may be moments of unbearable pain, accepting them, and then allowing them to make way for the inevitable moments of joy and happiness. Incorporating loss into life leads the way for that special brand of Israeli resilience.

While Sherri has described the very important role that social support played in her life, learning how to live alongside the grief and to find meaning in Koby's death came from the creation of the Koby Mandell Foundation. Without the daily visits of her friend and the strong togetherness with her husband, Sherri would have floundered, but this sense of mission gave Sherri's loss a direction and purpose and filled her days and nights with creative activity. Memorializing Koby in an active way that kept his name on the lips of many, not allowing him to be forgotten, was part of the healing process. Taking the pain of the loss and turning it into a creative endeavor helping first hundreds and by now thousands to heal from their own personal grief has brought a feeling of comfort to Sherri and her husband. Summer camps for kids, healing retreats for bereaved mothers and widows, and spiritual support groups are just a few of the activities that the Koby Mandell Foundation has promoted. For Sherri, knowing that much good has come out of the horror of her son's death allows her to continue living life to the fullest.

Sherri has touched death and returned to the living. She felt that each time she was at the edge of this bottomless pit, she was called back to life – by her children, by her friends, and by her community. When she advises people who have experienced a tragic loss, she tells them, reaching out from her own experience, "You will survive." She characterizes grief as a wild animal. It can come at you without warning and hit you when you are down. But you need to know that you will survive. In her final words of wisdom to us, she shares, "When you know death, you know life." This is an apt phrase from the mouth of a bereaved mother, born in the United States and now a full-fledged Israeli. This is the epitome of Israeli resilience.

CHAPTER 12

The Mayor of Rocket County

*"You always have to see the cup as half full.
I am a lucky guy."*

Gadi Yarkoni

Tell the World

The Palais des Nations in Geneva, Switzerland, is an imposing, historic building, housing the second-largest United Nations presence (after their headquarters in New York). Among other bodies, it is the base for the UN Human Rights Council, making the city a center for global human rights organizations, including the Red Cross. In a committee room overlooking Lake Geneva, three committee members sit in dark suits. Across from them sits an Israeli kibbutznik. It is the winter of 2015, the temperature that day dropping to 2°C (36°F). Yet, incongruously, the Israeli wears shorts with his work shirt. He looks like the typical kibbutznik that he is, but that is not why he is wearing shorts. He is wearing shorts because his legs were blown off six months earlier, the stumps are still healing, and he finds long pants uncomfortable. He has temporary prosthetics on both legs and uses a walker to ambulate. He is still in significant pain and has not yet completed his rehabilitation.

Half a year earlier, Gadi Yarkoni lost both his legs when a rocket landed between them. Israel was – to all intents and purposes – at war. It was the seventh and final week of Operation Protective Edge, a defensive military campaign launched by Israel in Gaza to counter a sustained rocket barrage toward Israel, which lost sixty-six soldiers and six civilians as the conflict played out. Earlier that day, a terrorist rocket had hit the power line carrying electricity to Kibbutz Nirim, where Yarkoni had been born and raised and was now part of the kibbutz management. He and two colleagues went out to fix the line. Gadi was unlucky – an hour before a ceasefire took hold, Hamas fired the rocket that exploded where he stood, less than fifteen seconds after the warning sirens sounded. There was nowhere to run. Yet Gadi considers himself lucky – he lost both his legs, but his colleagues – the kibbutz security coordinator Ze'ev Etzion and his deputy, Shahar Melamed – lost their lives in the attack.

When he was asked to fly to Geneva to give testimony to the United Nations Independent Commission of Inquiry on the 2014 Gaza Conflict, Gadi Yarkoni overcame initial hesitation and – accompanied by his wife – made the trip. Official Israel boycotted the commission, citing the bias of the controversial committee known for being steered by many human rights–abusing countries and for its relentless, disproportionate focus on Israel. Yet despite the pain and discomfort, Gadi's motivation in flying there was to articulate to the UN officials the unbearable reality of civilians living under fire – including Yarkoni's wife, his three daughters, his neighbors, and friends. He also wanted to make sure that the committee understood something that is so obvious to him: that the Israel Defense Forces are a moral fighting force, and that while there is sadly unintended collateral damage in war, the focus of IDF firepower is directed toward taking out terrorists, while the Hamas aim their weapons at civilians. If there had been no terror, there would have been no conflict.

Up for a Challenge

Several years after these events, we meet in the office of now mayor Gadi Yarkoni. The unpretentious office of the head of the Eshkol Regional Council is a modest building that is built of reinforced concrete to protect it from missile attacks. The regional council covers a triangular area of southern Israel between Ashkelon and Beersheba, with a border adjacent to both Egypt and the Gaza Strip. The latter has been run by Hamas since 2007, when an internal Palestinian conflict with the Fatah-run Palestinian Authority ignited a civil war between Gazans that saw hundreds killed.

Yarkoni experiences a certain amount of discomfort talking about his personal story and the attention he has received in recent years since his injury. While the limelight is no longer new to him, he feels more at ease when the focus of the discussion is on leadership, development, and working with the local population to create infrastructure, economic security, and quality of life. The region he oversees has been under continual rocket fire for two decades. There is the constant worry that terrorists are once again burrowing below residential homes as they seek to build more terror tunnels in order to kidnap and kill. PTSD cases are common in the children of this area. It is a physical and mental war of attrition. In some years, the rocket attacks are sporadic, but at times there are severe escalations: children stay home from school, and workplaces are shut down. When the situation will flare up again is anyone's guess. It is this reality that is wreaking havoc with the quality of life that Yarkoni is trying so hard to improve.

Despite this situation, Yarkoni exudes optimism and defiance when discussing life in his region surrounding Gaza, and even when he reflects on his injuries. That may be because the rocket attack that took his legs was not Yarkoni's first setback. Beginning back in 1985 when he was drafted into the IDF and was unable to serve as a combat soldier, Gadi has learned to deal with disappointments and setbacks of a physical nature. When he was diagnosed with glaucoma at age twenty-four and lost vision in one eye completely, with only limited vision in the remaining eye, Gadi had to make a life course correction and move from agricultural work in the fields that he loved so much to a different kind of employment where his remaining eyesight would be protected. Although schooling had never come easy for him, he decided that now was the time to make the maximal effort to study and prepare himself for a new career. In order to do that, he needed to complete his high school matriculation exams and get accepted to a college.

With much determination and hard work, Yarkoni successfully completed a college degree at Ruppin College, and upon return to the kibbutz took up various leadership positions, including director general of the kibbutz, a position he held for ten years. When he suffered a massive heart attack at age forty-two, his response was not to reduce his workload and take the easy path. To the contrary. Gadi added a neighboring kibbutz, Kisufim, to his work responsibilities, as he became the director of that kibbutz as well. He ran both kibbutzim, something virtually unheard of, for the next four years until the fateful day of his injury.

Gadi was not the only one giving testimony at the UN hearing in Geneva. Others included Gila Tragerman, the mother of four-year-old Daniel, who was killed in his home on Kibbutz Nahal Oz as a result of rocket fire, and Haim Yellin, then head of the Eshkol Regional Council. A longtime friend of Gadi's, he shared that he would be stepping down from his position in order to run for the Knesset, Israel's parliament, thus vacating this senior position. Gadi, who had never considered local politics before, began to think about whether this was a challenge he was up for. After consulting with his wife and some close friends, he decided to run and won, beating two other contenders to win 51 percent of the vote in the mayoral election. Currently Gadi is in his second term as council head, with no signs of stepping down or giving up the mantle.

A Lucky Guy

As Gadi tells his story, he shares about the fifteen days he was suspended between life and death. An unintended result of being intubated and put in a drug-induced coma immediately after his injury was that he missed the deep mourning the kibbutz members experienced for those they had lost, and he was not there with them to experience their great sense of disheartenment and loss of hope. This difficult period of time passed him by almost completely as he struggled for his life. When he awoke and was told by his wife about the death of his two friends, he knew that while it was important to remember them, it was even more important to carry on with more energy, more enthusiasm, and more spirit than ever before. As he began to heal in the rehab unit of Tel Hashomer Hospital, he continued to work, even though there were people replacing him in the day-to-day operations of the kibbutz. It is clear that being in control is an important feature of Gadi's leadership and likely a key feature of his ability to bounce back. He wants to know what is going on. He wants to be on the inside, to be part of the decision-making process, to be a mover and shaker, for all the right reasons.

When he heard that the position of head of council would soon be vacated, he began to see himself in that position in order to continue the momentum of his professional development. Till this day, he believes this is the antidote to sinking into depression, despair, and anxiety. He himself has never suffered symptoms of post-traumatic stress since his injury and the loss of his good friends who were standing right next to him. He does not – thankfully – appear to be wracked by "survivor's guilt," a common post-traumatic feeling experienced by those who live while others die. He clearly sees himself as a survivor, rather than a victim. He is sympathetic to others who suffer and maintains that what helps him, and the way he helps to encourage others, is focusing on the cup being half full. To that end, he remarked more than once how lucky he was that his amputations were both below the knee. Many would not see that as "luck," but Yarkoni expresses it with such sincerity that you believe him. No matter that he has two prosthetics. No matter that he still suffers from pain. He is a lucky guy, and he believes this with all his heart. He is alive to enjoy his family, his community, and his life.

When asked what else helped him heal aside from his innate optimism and his drive to lead and to create, he talks about his family and gets a bit misty-eyed. His wife, three children, two sisters, and parents showered him with constant visits during his long rehabilitation, despite the distances (a good two-hour trip in each direction). He notes that his family has become much closer since his injury, for which he is very thankful.

How do you build resilience in the population of the south of Israel that has been under rocket attacks for twenty years? How do you blunt the psychological impact of the constant yet unpredictable red alert sirens, the never-ending sounds of rocket fire, and the resulting carnage from attacks? Gadi seems incredibly resilient, and we can learn from him two important principles: optimism and activity. Gadi doesn't sit still and doesn't wait for things to happen. He is clearly in the driver's seat. He is in charge; he controls, initiates, and directs. Much of this is inborn or imbibed from a very early age from his parents and other people who influenced Gadi, as well as from the generation of kibbutzniks he represents. When looking at the younger generation, whose entire childhood has been spent in the shadow of rocket attacks, we often see a different story, a more nuanced and complicated one.

For example, the percentage of children and young adults who have grown up in the area bordering Gaza and suffer from post-traumatic stress symptoms is exceptionally high. The levels of anxiety reported by parents and children alike is similarly extreme. This is not surprising, despite the existence of resilience centers for treatment and the proliferation of "safe rooms" and shelters in most houses and community buildings. The sheer number of rockets that has fallen over the last twenty years erodes feelings of security and safety and makes resilience hard to come by.

Gadi Yarkoni is a shining light in this often troubled setting and works hard at keeping up morale for the entire community. His emphasis on economic development and growth, his dynamism, and his enthusiastic optimism are magnetic. This is not only central to his being, but explains in large part how he has overcome the challenges that life has dealt him. He believes that in order to live in this part of Israel, one must be convinced that the current situation will not go on forever, and that the rocket fire will cease one day. Peace may be elusive, yet his hope that the citizens of both Israel and Gaza will be able to coexist, without warfare, reigns strong. The mayor of rocket county is an eternal optimist.

CHAPTER 13

The Climb

"In the airless void, the only thing that stands between you and death is yourself: your wits, your preparation, your mental and physical strength."

Nadav Ben Yehuda,
AIPAC Policy Conference, 2013

Pushing the Limits

It was a high-altitude engagement. They had met as students, and Nadav introduced Lena to climbing, which she grew to love. The mountain-top marriage proposal had been in the planning for quite some time. Any major climb takes meticulous months of organizing, but in addition to preparing for change of weather or potential injury, Nadav needed to prepare for Lena's answer. At the summit of Kilimanjaro, there was just enough oxygen to say a yes or no. Demonstrating clearly his thoroughness of character, Nadav had brought two rings with him up the mountain. One was his mother's and one his grandmother's. Neither of them were actually for his potential fiancée to keep, but they were of different sizes, and Nadav assumed that at least one of the rings would work for the proposal, before choosing the perfect ring for her back home. Fortunately, Lena said yes, and Nadav removed her glove, baring her hand to the -20°C (-4°F) cold just long enough to put the ring on. Due to inclement weather conditions, they were unable to communicate their happy news to friends and family for a few days. To the blissful ignorance of the outside world, the climbers were engaged!

Everyone has peaks and troughs in life, but few get to experience the highest of highs as Nadav Ben Yehuda has. He is the Israeli who has climbed the most mountains above eight thousand meters (twenty-six thousand feet), and he is the first Israeli to climb Annapurna I, the deadliest mountain on the planet. He also made the first Israeli winter ascent of the highest mountain in Europe, and holds the record as the Israeli champion of Skyscrapers Stair Climbing. Nadav's story is all about pushing the limits of human potential and moving forward despite setbacks, meeting challenges head on.

Nadav is tall and engaging, with a deep voice and a kind face. Appropriately enough, he was born to a family living on a mountain – in Jerusalem. Later his family moved to the city of Rehovot in the central plains of Israel, south of Tel Aviv. He is the oldest child in his family, followed by two sisters and two brothers. His parents met on Kibbutz Merom Golan in northern Israel. Nadav, their firstborn, always had an outdoorsy kibbutz spirit and a strong connection to nature. Whenever Nadav's parents had some savings to spare, rather than buy furniture or appliances, they took the family to travel abroad. Thus, young Nadav traveled in several remote places, exposing him to landscapes and terrain that looked very different from his native Israel.

Nadav recalls seeing his first "real" mountain in Chamonix, France, when he was about eight years old. Nadav stood on tiptoe to peer out of the cable car window. While everyone else's eyes were on Mont Blanc, "the white lady," Nadav was transfixed by the glacier below. From his tiptoe perch, he managed to make out dots that looked like tiny pixels in a picture. They were in fact mountain climbers. His mind was afire to know not simply why they climb, but rather practically how they climb. The sense of challenge and direct connection to nature fascinated him and led to his eventual lifelong devotion to ice climbing.

Nadav began his own climbing career during his teens. He started by going down, rather than up, utilizing ropes as a method of transport. He practiced rappelling, canyoneering, caving, and river crossing, then started rock climbing, eventually focusing on alpine, mixed, and ice climbing, in addition to high-altitude mountaineering. Those ropes would become central to his life. Nadav enlisted for his mandatory IDF service, which was an intensive one, serving in the Sayeret Golani special forces unit as a combat soldier, acting operations officer, and combat team commander. Nadav continues to do reserve duty in the Special Forces Alpinist Unit. Looking back on his service, Nadav notes that when the army wants to train you, you carry someone on your back; when they want to teach you a lesson, you carry someone on your back; in order to receive a reward, you carry someone on your back. Looking out for one another and extracting your comrade from danger is a lesson well learned and a value that would become a tenet of Nadav Ben Yehuda's life.

Living on the Edge

Nadav says he believes in love at first sight. This was true of his wife Lena, and this is true of mountains as well. He falls in love with mountains the first time he sees them. His relationship with climbing, on the other hand, he defines as a love-hate one. You embark on a journey that you really are looking forward to, and you have chosen to do, but the cost is great. First there is the actual financial cost, which is substantial. Add to that a mental cost, a physical cost, a medical cost, and a cost to family life, and you can begin to understand the complex nature of this profession. Nadav Ben Yehuda has experienced and endured all of these costs, multiple times.

Nadav's entire life is about mountains. His wall is adorned with a giant map. He places a pin in it to select his next climb and then begins to research. With a vocation such as ice climbing, preparation and training are key, but the only real way to do this is on the ice – and Israel does not have a single glacier to train on. This requires several months a year of training abroad, and every mountain, icefall, or crag that he climbs is also a preparation for the next one. There are no shortcuts to climbing. You must take into account the risks as well as your skill level and ability to make the climb. Mental preparation – visualization, as Ben Yehuda terms it – is critical. You have to think and even dream about the mountain so much so that when you eventually get there, it feels like déjà vu. Photos and intelligence gathered by other climbers play an important part here. Despite the intensive days, weeks, and months of planning, the actual terrain is never exactly what one had imagined. Unlike rock climbing, the face of an icy mountain changes on a daily basis, and the surprises involved are part of the project. Once the climb begins, Nadav describes his single-minded concentration as he enters a state of mental hardiness that allows him to focus solely on his mission, shielding thoughts of family, friends, sea-level concerns or luxuries, and of the perils involved in a "safe zone" within his mind.

In 2016, Nadav became the first Israeli to ascend the deadliest mountain in the world, Annapurna I (8,091 meters or 26,545 feet) – which has a more than 30 percent death rate for those attempting the climb. He climbed for almost seventy days. The night after this exhausting climb, Nadav recalls falling asleep, enveloped in his hotel room bed in Kathmandu, only to wake up hours later with feverish nightmares of dangerous, life-threatening scenarios. After closing off his consciousness to these thoughts for over two months, he was suddenly beset by them. Fear, says Nadav, is an important part of climbing: "If I meet a person who is not afraid of a climb, I am immediately afraid of them."

Most people live out their lives within a safe zone. Nadav lives within a danger zone, literally on the edge. The truth is, he says confidently, that he is not a risk taker, and when it comes to climbing, he works relentlessly to minimize, mitigate, and avoid dangers. There is a spectrum between making conservative choices and taking risks. Nadav does not view himself nor what he does as extreme. He does not gamble, drink coffee or alcohol, eat salt or sweets, smoke, or do drugs – all to keep his body and mind oriented to his goals. Nadav looks at things scientifically and assesses the likelihood of potential for danger. He is not reckless. He is literally, as goes the Hebrew phrase for a science nerd, a "good boy from Jerusalem." Nevertheless, in climbing, as in life, there is always an element of the unknown. You cannot predict every eventuality or be 100 percent confident about everything. Being at peace with that fact allows you to live outside your comfort zone and to take on new challenges with confidence.

In a life of shifting ice fields, instability is a constant. It is the predictable unpredictability that prevents Nadav from having a clear timeline of upcoming climbs. There are so many variables to consider. A country might close its borders, permits may be withheld, or a cardinal serac (a column of glacial ice) may break on one particular mountain. As a result, Nadav has learned to be flexible, but once he has decided on an objective, he fully commits. That commitment is imperative, as there will always be good excuses to be found for not attempting a given climb.

The Moment of Truth

Nadav started eyeing the highest mountain in the world a few years before attempting to climb it. Preparation was hard and lengthy. Mount Everest (8,848 meters or 29,029 feet) was a challenge he wanted to take on, but Nadav did not see it as an end in itself – he wanted to climb in the world of the eight-thousanders, the nickname for the fourteen mountains above eight thousand meters (26,427 feet). Climbing Everest takes months. In preparation, you have to acclimatize in different altitudes for the low oxygen levels and to understand the intrinsic logistics needed for this vast Himalayan ascent. In addition to heavy high-altitude climbing gear on your body, such as a down suit, crampons, ice axes, and a helmet, the equipment list goes on and on. Even if you get your own preparation right, you are still in the hands of much larger and uncontrollable forces, such as glacial movements, avalanche risk, and meteorological states, all making it very clear that reaching a summit is never guaranteed.

The year 2012 was a controversial time for Everest, which experienced one of the busiest seasons in its history. This prompted fears that commercialization would lead to inexperienced climbers attempting a climb that they were not ready for. In addition to committed climbers like Nadav, there are those adventurers or attempted record breakers who see Everest as something to check off a bucket list. Climbing Everest is an expensive undertaking. Just the cost for the permit alone is between $11,000 and $18,000 (and constantly rising) per climber, and that is before the additional costs for logistics, gear, insurance, and the climb itself, which can run into additional tens of thousands of dollars. It is also dangerous. Toward the summit of Mount Everest lie more than two hundred dead bodies. Without proper training, posing for that precious photo at the summit could be one of the most expensive and dangerous selfies you ever take. Plenty do, however, bear the expense and take the risk.

One such person was a Turkish climber whom Nadav met on his way to the mountain. Despite having no climbing experience at all, he wanted to be the first person in the world to scale Mount Everest, as the first mountain in his life, while holding a bicycle. Later on, he would be arrested for attempting this stunt; a showman at heart, he had threatened to set himself and the camp on fire with cans of kerosene if anyone touched his bike. In the end, both he and his bicycle were removed from the mountain by the authorities, an action he accused of being a Nepali government conspiracy against him. As Nadav would later find out, this did not deter the Turkish climber from reattempting the climb, with serious repercussions for Nadav as well.

It happened as Nadav was just about three hundred meters (a thousand feet) below the summit. He had already encountered two dead bodies on the last part of the climb, and his apprehension of the consequences of too many inexperienced climbers on the mountain was being confirmed before his eyes. Then he saw another body that at first glance appeared to be dead. It was the Turk he had met on the way to the mountain. He was in a very bad way, but still alive. He had no oxygen equipment and was injured and unable to speak. He was a total mess, with no backpack, gloves, or ice axes. In Nadav's words, it looked like "he was waiting for the end." Nadav was furious that someone would place himself and other climbers at a significantly higher risk due to his lack of preparedness for the climb. As a result, Nadav now needed to make an instantaneous decision, one that would prove fateful: climb up and become the youngest Israeli to reach the summit of Mount Everest, or give up when he was so close to the top in order to help a stranger in distress, while imperiling his own life, too.

This was no dilemma for Nadav. There was no doubt in his mind about what he needed to do. Nadav decided to abort his own climb just about three hundred meters short of the summit in order to try to lower the injured person down the mountain alive. Nadav attached him to his own harness between his legs via a short-rope, loading both their weights on the rope systems, using his legs to traverse horizontally and his hands to control the vertical descent, while maneuvering with the additional gravitational pull of the injured man. On the way down, Nadav's own oxygen system broke, and he needed to constantly remove his gloves in temperatures of tens of degrees below zero so he could operate the systems. Not long after, his right hand completely froze and ceased to function. It took eight hours for Nadav and the Turk – who was flitting in and out of consciousness – to get to the highest camp. Periodically assisted by other climbers along the way, the descent continued to a lower glacier at an elevation where a helicopter could land.

Nadav himself was severely injured during the descent, leaving him with orthopedic disorders, injuries to his feet, hands, and face, and drastic weight loss throughout the climb and rescue (nineteen kilograms, nearly forty-two pounds). The helicopter brought them to safety, and medical care was at hand. When Nadav was finally seen by doctors, they wanted to immediately amputate four of the fingers from his right hand. He flatly refused, insisting on fighting for his hand; his fingers, while not perfect, remain quite functional today. Both Nadav and the person he saved survived, and over time, recovered, relatively. Looking back, Nadav explains that the decision he made whether to reach the summit or save a life was instantaneous. Subsequent to that first decision there were a series of additional decisions, each one life threatening, with the need to constantly assess whether by making the dangerous descent together, they would survive or whether it would kill one or both of them.

This event attracted a lot of attention from the international media, and for the first time, Nadav found himself unwillingly in the spotlight. Since the person that Nadav, the Israeli, had saved was Turkish, and those two countries were diplomatically at odds, the media gave the coverage a geopolitical slant. They posed for photos with their flags, and the Turk thanked Nadav in multiple interviews and videos for saving his life. He called Nadav's mother to thank her, telling her they now have family in Turkey too. However, later on, pressure got to him, and the man Nadav saved changed his story. He subsequently claimed that he was never rescued at all, particularly by an "Israeli soldier," and that he was a victim of an Israeli conspiracy against him as a Turkish national. He began to rail against the Jewish state, defaming Israel with some of the worst allegations made by anti-Israel organizations. This was difficult for Nadav, who loves Turkey and the Turkish people. While the world saw an act of humanity, which not only cost Nadav reaching the summit, but more importantly severely endangered his life, no one expected it to become politicized. Up until that moment, Nadav's experience within the climbing community was one in which borders did not exist. Nadav has friends from many countries that do not maintain diplomatic relations with Israel, and this has never been a problem.

Two months after the life-threatening rescue, while Nadav was still undergoing intensive rehabilitation, he received a phone call from the office of the president of Israel, Shimon Peres. He was to be awarded the Israel Presidential Medal of Honor. He also received an honorary medal from the president of Florida International University. In the following years, he was given the Best Athlete in the Alpine Climbing Field award by the Israeli Federation for Non-Olympic Competitive Sports and was chosen by *Forbes* magazine as one of the most influential people under the age of thirty.

Despite the unsought adulation, recovery was tough, and Nadav's fingers were still blackened from frostbite for months later. He had frostbite in four fingers on his right hand and several toes, and he had damaged sensation and mobility in his left hand. Many medical procedures ensued. With the support of his family and doctors, he recuperated and slowly returned to climbing, but Nadav did not return to the Himalayas for sixteen months, a frustratingly long time for him to be away from his passion. When he finally did return to the big mountains, it was to the eighth highest mountain in the world, Manaslu, Nepal, which means "mountain of the spirit." It was cathartic for him get back into thin air.

Back in the Saddle

The story picks up again in 2014, when Nadav Ben Yehuda was returning home from Tibet, having concluded an eight-thousand-meter climb. He was contacted by the Israeli Ministry of Foreign Affairs. There had been a severe snowstorm caused by a massive cyclone in the Indian Ocean during the busy trekking season in Nepal, which is one of the destinations that young Israelis enjoy visiting as part of their post-army trips. The Israeli embassy in Kathmandu had been alerted about Israeli trekkers who were trapped on a mountain pass. The stranded Israeli trekkers had written a note in Hebrew, which they attached to a mule led by a local porter who managed to descend the mountain pass to a nearby village. The message was then communicated to the embassy.

Israeli search and rescue teams flew out to Nepal to help find the survivors of the blizzard. Due to high altitudes they would experience during the rescue attempts, the teams would need time to acclimatize to the heights, whereas Nadav was already acclimatized. He was asked to join the search and rescue efforts, and immediately agreed to embark on various missions across the great Himalayan ranges of Everest, Langtang, and Annapurna. A year later, in late April 2015, Nadav joined the embassy of Nepal in Israel to coordinate rescue missions and humanitarian support, while assisting Israel's Foreign Ministry to trace missing Israeli citizens immediately following the massive earthquakes in Nepal.

There is an innate loneliness to mountaineering. However much support one might have, it is your individual hands and feet that make their way from crag to dangerous crag. Nadav is fortunate to have teams and the operations center of logistics, meteorology, and rescues managed by Lena, who is a very important partner in his achievements. The perseverance and stamina needed to continue comes from both inner reserves and also from knowing that there are a lot of people willing you on, from thousands of feet below you or thousands of miles away.

There is also great comfort and strength in knowing that if you are in danger, those people would come to your aid.

Following the snowstorm rescue effort, Nadav was asked by an American tourist why there were so many Israelis in Kathmandu assisting with the search effort. In response, he showed him the front page of one of the most popular Hebrew news websites, reporting on another rescue effort happening at the same time in Peru. A handful of Israelis were missing following a rafting accident – it was being reported as a major disaster. The story had been front-page news for several days. Whereas in many countries of the world, a few lost tourists might be considered a minor story, in Israel, this merits headline news, because each Israeli is a "brother" or "sister." The ethos drawn from the Talmudic proverb that "all Israel is responsible one for the other" is something learned early in life and engraved on the hearts of even the toughest Israelis.

In 2018, Nadav attempted Kangchenjunga, the third highest and one of the most difficult mountains in the world, soaring at 8,586 meters (28,110 feet), located in the Himalayas, between Nepal and India. It was his second try at the climb. One year earlier, Nadav had climbed to 8,150 meters, the highest point achieved for several years on Kangchenjunga. Following that, it was time for the next challenge: he set out to climb another eight-thousander in a bid to see how quickly he could make it from sea level to summit without the use of supplemental oxygen or any pre-acclimatization. He managed that potentially months-long climb in just fourteen days, and then decided to go back to Kangchenjunga for a second attempt in the next season of 2018.

This time, Nadav reached the highest point among any of the few climbers who did not use supplemental oxygen. But about 140 meters below the summit, due to changing conditions, Nadav decided to turn back, a difficult decision to make on one of the hardest mountain faces in the world. It was on this descent that disaster struck, and he fell.

He was so badly injured that he stayed above eight thousand meters at temperatures of tens of degrees below zero, still without an oxygen system, for an additional twenty-four hours, unable to climb down, relentlessly trying to move himself a few centimeters at a time. Fellow climbers who had lost contact with him transmitted multiple times via voice communicators that Nadav had perished, and they decided to descend the mountain. Nadav was left for dead in the "death zone."

But he survived and managed to get himself down the mountain with the help of friends from all over the world, as part of a complicated and formidable multi-day extraction – and now he is recovering. With a broken and necrotic body, Nadav has undergone multiple operations, including amputation surgeries, and now walks with crutches. This is a marked improvement from when he was confined first to an isolated ICU bed and then to a wheelchair, for more than a year. But life is stronger than anything, and Nadav keeps moving forward. During his recovery, Nadav was appointed a Goodwill Ambassador by the government of Nepal, promoting links between the two countries he considers his home: Israel and Nepal. While he plans his way back to the mountains and rehabilitates his body, Nadav spends his time also developing his mind and his curiosity: in addition to his past two bachelor degrees, he completed an MPH in emergency and disaster management at Tel Aviv University, and is studying for an MSc in extreme medicine at Exeter University. He is working on his PhD proposal in medical sciences and lectures about his fields of expertise around the world.

Several years after Nadav's mountaintop proposal to Lena, there is a newcomer on the scene. Newborn baby Adam is cooing and gurgling as he heads off for an afternoon nap, while we continue the interview. It is clear that Nadav is besotted with his son. Yet minutes later he is once again consumed with talking about his previous expeditions. This is the restless life of a climber: when you are in the mountains, you want to be back with your family, and when you are at home, you want to be back in the mountains. Nadav underscores that those are different types of love, both filling his heart with happiness and fulfillment. Even when you are feeling low, you set your sights high, and the sky is not the limit.

Nadav is used to working under conditions in which the next step you take can literally be the difference between life and death. Most of us do not crave these challenges, nor do we find ourselves in a freezing, high-altitude environment with a paucity of breathable air. But climbing, like life, is predicated on a series of consequences and decisions, and there is much to learn from Nadav's story. The consequences, we have no control over; but when it comes to the decisions, we do have total control. Flexibility, one of the keys to resilience, is a vital coping mechanism for unknown terrain – whether on a mountain or in our daily lives. It allows us to make clear-eyed decisions, as it did for Nadav on the day he set aside his goal to reach Everest's summit and instead chose to save a life.

CHAPTER 14

National Resilience

"What Israelis can teach the world is that life goes on, despite terrible things. And I think that's a wonderful message."

Colonel (Res.) Miri Eisin

A Time of Terror

During the late 1990s and early 2000s, Israel was suffering an ongoing period of terror attacks that were overwhelming in their sheer number, their gruesomeness, and the toll they took on human life. The number of Israelis murdered and maimed by terrorists reached a peak in 2002, with over double the fatalities of the previous year. The terrorists' methods and targets were myriad: snipers, roadside bombs, suicide terrorists, shootings, vehicle rammings, and stabbings took place on civilian roads, in restaurants, buses, shopping malls, discotheques, and even an ice cream parlor and pizzeria. Israelis girded themselves on a daily basis for the next breaking news report telling of where the latest carnage had taken place. As always, the conflict made headlines on news networks the world over. That year, for the first time, the internationally recognized public face of the Israel Defense Forces was a woman. In

131

2002, Colonel Miri Eisin was thrust from her behind-the-scenes role into the glare of the media limelight as the new IDF Spokesperson to the international media.

Colonel Eisin was ready for the challenge. Born in the United States, she moved with her parents to Israel when she was a child. Eisin's English was fluent, and she spoke in clear, empathetic tones. After graduating high school in 1980, she joined the IDF and was accepted into officers' training in the Intelligence Corps. Eisin served for more than twenty years in the Military Intelligence Directorate of the IDF in a variety of field and research positions, across the tenure of several different generals. Positions she held included deputy head of combat intelligence and personal assistant to the director of military intelligence.

This allowed her the privilege of being the proverbial fly on the wall to important matters of state and privy to many critical military discussions. As adjunct to the chief of staff, Eisin sat in Israeli government cabinet meetings chaired by successive prime ministers. Miri is one of a small cohort of people who can summon twenty-five years of insider's knowledge as to how decisions are made in the Israeli cabinet relating to military assessments and national readiness planning. Retiring as a full colonel, Eisin is also one of the tiny group of Israeli women to achieve that rank in the military (fewer than 2 percent of colonels are female).

Having previously been a military spokesperson, Eisin entered her new role in government in 2002 as the prime minister's foreign media advisor following a particularly brutal and symbolically painful terror attack, the Seder night massacre at the Park Hotel. The beachfront promenade of Netanya, a seaside town thirty minutes north of Tel Aviv, is typically a serene place on a spring evening, with both local residents and tourists out strolling alongside the sea. On that particular night, few were walking the boardwalk, as it was the first night of Passover.

When it comes to observing the Jewish calendar, there are two dates during the year that the vast majority of Israelis commemorate dutifully, whether they are religious or not. They are the Yom Kippur fast and the Passover Seder. On the night of March 27, 2002, hundreds of guests were gathered to observe the holiday by partaking in their Seder meal in the large dining room at the hotel, looking forward to a night spent celebrating together with their family members, young and old.

Abdel-Basset Odeh had other plans. The twenty-five-year-old Palestinian terrorist affiliated with Hamas disguised himself as a woman and walked into the hotel carrying a powerful bomb inside a suitcase. Managing to avoid detection by the security guard, he detonated the explosive, turning the traditional holiday feast into a scene of carnage. In an instant, twenty-eight people were killed by the blast and over 140 were injured, many seriously. Two more people subsequently died of their injuries. It was later discovered that Hamas had planned to use both cyanide and chlorine nerve agents during this attack, as well, but fortunately for some unknown reason they did not make it to the bomber. The majority of those murdered were over the age of seventy; they included survivors of the Holocaust, family patriarchs and matriarchs, and young children. The oldest victim was ninety years old.

Even for a nation that had become accustomed to terror attacks, the ensuing images were stomach churning. The symbolism of the massacre taking place at Passover was a gut-punch to Jews worldwide. Within days, the IDF responded to the bloodshed with Operation Defensive Shield – the largest military operation in the West Bank since the Six-Day War in 1967. The goal was to root out terror cells and put an end to the heinous attacks. The operation lasted over a month, beginning with placing Palestinian Authority leader Yasser Arafat under siege while Israeli forces confiscated enormous quantities of weapons and arrested terrorist leaders.

The Public Face of Israel

Against this backdrop, Colonel Miri Eisin made a move that few have, leaving the anonymity of her role in military intelligence to become the new public face of Israel to the world. TV news broadcasts have rarely been willing to give Israel the benefit of the doubt, and Eisin, new to the job, found herself on the receiving end of many a hostile interview. She represented Israel's position with poise and a no-nonsense manner, yet was able to show concern and empathy toward unintended Palestinian casualties during the campaign. Eisin went on to consistently represent Israel's point of view to CNN, the BBC, the Associated Press, and multiple other networks.

When her husband, a lieutenant colonel at the time, was accepted to the Wexner program at Harvard University, Miri left together with their three children under the age of five to live in Boston for the duration of the school year. While there, she addressed a wide variety of audiences on issues relating to Israel, security, and public diplomacy. By the time Eisin returned to Israel, events had rocked Israeli politics. In January 2006, Prime Minister Ariel Sharon, who led the evacuation of Israeli communities from Gaza a year earlier, suffered a sudden, debilitating stroke. His successor was the former mayor of Jerusalem, Ehud Olmert.

The mettle of the new prime minister was tested early. On June 25, 2006, a group of terrorists from Gaza, comprising members of the Izz ad-Din al-Qassam Brigades, Popular Resistance Committees, and Army of Islam, crossed into Israel via an underground tunnel and attacked an IDF post. They killed two Israeli soldiers, wounded another two, and kidnapped a young IDF corporal by the name of Gilad Schalit. Within weeks, tensions rose to the north of Israel, as well. Following the unilateral withdrawal of forces from Southern Lebanon in 2000, Israel's northern border had remained relatively quiet for years, but inside Lebanon, the Hezbollah terrorist organization was growing stronger by the day. Steadily, they became part of Lebanon's political scene, yet all the while, with significant funding from both Syria and Iran, they invested heavily in rockets pointed toward Israel and a complex infrastructure of bunkers, anti-tank and anti-ship missiles. On July 12, 2006, Hezbollah carried out a cross-border attack, ambushing two IDF patrol vehicles inside the Israeli border. They killed two soldiers and injured two more, while taking two others – Ehud Goldwasser and Eldad Regev – hostage.

The IDF retaliated with a large campaign, which carried through the summer of 2006, later becoming known as the Second Lebanon War. In the new internet era, where social media was beginning to take hold and cable news was 24/7, Prime Minister Olmert needed urgent help with Israel's public relations and the image Israel presented to the world. He requested that Eisin become his personal international media advisor. She was initially reluctant, but with an abiding sense of duty, she agreed to do this on an interim basis. After several months, she was asked by the prime minister to continue. The first female in this position, Eisin was a reassuring TV presence, calm, clear, and eloquent, strong, yet sympathetic. Reflecting on her performance during the conflict, Eisin stated, "I don't expect to win the media war, but I don't intend to lose. We have managed to hold our own with our messages."

Most official spokespeople have been men, many of whom stood before television cameras in uniform. Eisin gave the government line but also showed heart for casualties on the "other side," for instance, Lebanese who found themselves in the firing line due to Hezbollah fighters deliberately embedding themselves in communities in order to utilize them as human shields. She was also unflappable. Despite constantly being tested by TV news anchors who oftentimes would rage at Israel via its spokesperson, Miri maintained her cool. Frequently the framing of the story being told abroad was that Israel – rather than

Hezbollah or Hamas – was the aggressor. This made Eisin even more determined to portray her country on visual media in empathetic terms and not as overly bellicose or hardline. The result often had audiences questioning the tone of the questioner rather than that of the person answering the questions.

The aftermath of the Second Lebanon War saw international criticism of Israel as well as a flurry of diplomatic activity aimed at bringing the conflict to a halt. Eisin continued by the prime minister's side serving as the voice of Olmert's administration to the world media as he headed to Maryland for the 2007 Annapolis Peace Conference with the Palestinians, hosted by President George W. Bush. Since becoming Israel's spokesperson in war and in peace negotiations, Eisin has extensively lectured on issues relating to her previous work in the IDF and on the skill involved in crafting and framing Israel's message. Given her unique background, she is perfectly placed to reflect on issues related to Israelis' internal sense of resilience in the face of a never-ending and multifaceted conflict.

Shaped by Service

While Miri Eisen's personal resilience is huge, her perspective on the national character of Israel – and resilience as a characteristic of the national psyche – is unique and powerful.

One of the facts of life for those living in Israel is that military service is compulsory. A narrow sliver of land in a neighborhood of rogue regimes and terror groups and always under threat, Israel requires most of its eighteen-year old citizens, both male and female, to enlist. Eisin contends that this service will likely be the most significant thing that people do in their lives and speaks to a sense of service to a greater cause, of which Israelis are overwhelmingly proud. While for the majority, this is a hugely positive experience, for some it can take a toll, whether via physical or emotional injury.

Speaking as both an IDF colonel and as a mother, Eisin talks of the unwritten contract between the state and its parents. Parents understand that this service may require exposing their children to unsafe environments, but are reassured that the country promises to do everything it can to bring their offspring back home safely. You can see it on the faces of parents on the child's conscription day: a mixture of pride and concern. That demonstrates the fraught and complex nature of this unwritten contract, to which both sides are, for the most part, willing partners. Parents are expected to do everything they can to support and facilitate their children going to the army. Eisin puts it this way: "As a mother, I want my kid to be safe. As a citizen, I want my country to be safe." It is an intensely sensitive topic, but Israelis take it as a given – part of the socialization of Israeli society. In a very real sense, it is not just the eighteen-year-old "kids" who are enlisting; the parents of those "kids" are being drafted too. In recent decades, parents have become more involved, and the military has become more understanding that they need to give responses to parental concerns.

As a colonel, Miri Eisin's sense is that the IDF is a place that gives young adults the chance to do things that are amazing at that period of life. It provides them with the kind of responsibility or authority that few other countries offer people of that age. It is, she says, part of the reason that Israel has been termed a "start-up nation." Conscription age, somewhere between eighteen and twenty, comes at a time when brains are developing and capabilities are being honed, but in most places, this is also the age when formal education ends, even while brain development continues. So, at a stage when most countries send young people to college or out into the workforce, Israel is putting them into a very stressful environment but giving them authority and responsibility as well as a framework and a purpose. It was that sense of service that attracted Eisin to remain inside a structure that she feels gives people a variety of ways to serve and allows people within it to be innovative and to create change.

Eisin also considers it important that Israelis are exposed to responsibility and authority at a relatively young age. She contends that the phrase "young adults" does not really exist in Israel, because at the age of consent, Israelis are thrust into a strict hierarchy for a number of years. When they are released from the army, they are already several years older than those who are just starting out in most other countries.

On the flip side, while their peers elsewhere are deciding for themselves what to do and making active choices about their future, Israelis are being told what to do. They are assigned a position, and although they can express a preference, it is not always accommodated. They have someone, usually only a year or two older than them, telling them what to do day in, day out. The military has its own set of priorities, and it is the military that decides how and where to utilize the skill set of each conscript, whether the individual is happy about that choice or not. This combination of being given real responsibility in an environment that puts a value on innovation and flexibility means that the students walking onto university campuses following their IDF service are older and of a different caliber compared to first-year students around the world. The army experience teaches the importance of both flexibility and of meaning, two key components for building resilience.

The Survivor Mentality

Our discussion with Eisin takes place just prior to Holocaust Memorial Day, and in her mind, the Holocaust looms large in the collective memory of the nation. Internationally, Holocaust Memorial Day is observed on January 27 – the anniversary of the liberation of Auschwitz – but in Israel, Yom Hashoah is on the date of the Warsaw Ghetto Uprising to celebrate defiance in the face of tyranny while commemorating the victims of tyranny's slaughter. The Israeli psyche is heavily influenced by a feeling of post-traumatic stress. Not only have Israelis experienced gargantuan traumas in their recent history, but there is a constant feeling that their backs are against the wall, prompting them to say, "We will survive because history has taught us that we *must* survive." Eisin notes an interesting contrast. She remarks that Israelis give a large amount of freedom to their children, as if to counter the fact that the region is a dangerous one. Israel is a child-friendly society and there is a low rate of street crime, allowing Israeli children to freely ride the bus and go out independently day and night. Their resilience and strength is built by having a greater level of personal freedom at a relatively young age.

Israelis also feel they belong to a community – whether on a national scale or locally via their city, kibbutz, village, school, or synagogue. Beyond work and family, that sense of community gives citizens cohesiveness, resilience, and a sense of being "in it together." As a result, they also feel the pain of loss of each and every soldier, and each and every terror victim, whether they knew them personally or not. The nation grieves together too. Citing the 2014 Hamas kidnapping of three Israeli teens that gripped the national psyche of Israelis for weeks, Eisin points to the way that kidnapping affected the collective. These were everyone's kids. When someone in the community gets hurt, everyone hurts.

Israelis are also notably thick-skinned; their tough exterior has become something of a national characteristic. Eisin cites the fact that modern-day Israel is a *kibbutz galuyot* of identities – using the biblical term for "the ingathering of the exiles." For millennia, this was the prayer of Jews around the globe, dispersed in an ongoing exile from Israel, longing to reunite once more with the smaller number of Jews who never left the Holy Land and with the land itself. An early piece of legislation passed by Israel's parliament following the reestablishment of the modern Jewish state was the Law of Return, giving Jews worldwide the automatic right to obtain Israeli citizenship. Today, Israel's Jewish population is a polyglot of languages, cultures, and birthplaces from Russia to Ethiopia, from Iraq to Australia, and everything in between.

Among the many who immigrated to modern Israel, a large number were from nondemocratic countries where they faced great adversity. This is something that plays into the Israeli national character but also makes it all the more interesting that there was never any doubt in 1948 that Israel would be a liberal democracy. That Israel has been able to absorb and bring together such a tapestry of peoples is a modern-day miracle. While challenges abound, that unity – which is prevalent around so many issues of national identity and security – builds into an essential resilience firewall.

Returning to her personal resilience, Miri is no longer part of the rough-and-tumble that went along with representing official Israel, but she reflects on her time in front of the cameras. There are particular tensions between the type of job she was in – both in the military and as a government representative – that are often harder for a working mother than for her male counterparts. The job took its toll on family life. Eisin admits that she often considered resigning, but she could not say no to the prime minister and to her country.

While representing her country to ABC, Fox, MSNBC, and others during the Second Lebanon War, Eisin was mother to three children under the age of seven. She recalls returning home from a particularly grueling day at the office, and, as frequently happened, work spilled over into home life, and she was speaking on the phone to the prime minister in the evening. Yael, Eisin's then six-year-old daughter, wanted her mother's attention, but Miri gestured her away so she could finish the conversation with the Israeli premier. Aware that she could not make a noise due to the importance of the person on the other end of the phone line, but unable to suppress her need for attention, Yael silently sobbed. Seeing that made it clear to Eisin that it was time to leave her job and move on.

Now in civilian life for over a decade, Israel's spokesperson has cultivated her own voice. In her current, "unofficial" capacity, she remains connected to the security establishment and is briefed regularly on public diplomacy. Yet with the freedom and balance that being a freelancer gives her, she feels that she is a better representative of the country she loves than when she was doing so as an official. She also has a clear perspective on Israel's national character: "When I think about resilience," she says, "I think that what Israelis can teach the world is that life goes on, despite the terrible things that happen. That's a wonderful message – it's a survivor's message, not a victim's message. The day after a terror attack is a regular day when you send your kids back to school. We take a deep breath and carry on. That's resilience."

Afterword

*"Everything can be taken from a man, but one thing: the last of the
human's human freedoms – to choose one's attitude in any given set of
circumstances, to choose one's own way."*
Viktor E. Frankl, Man's Search for Meaning

Given the very real danger of regional instability coupled with ongoing and constant threats of destruction by its neighbors, by any rational analysis, Israel should not exist at all, let alone be a thriving powerhouse of a country. Yet as we rediscovered via the personalities we met on this journey, Israel defies reason, logic, and historical precedent, and these amazing Israelis embody the wonder that their country represents.

Even in peacetime – or to give it the Hebrew vernacular, *shigrah* (routine) – Israelis are under great stress. The threat to Israel's existence is ever present and often manifests itself without warning. One does not need to dwell on history to see this in action: terror attacks are unfortunately far too commonplace in modern-day Israel. Yet life goes on, and people are not just living day to day but making long-term plans as well.

Is resilience a product of nature or nurture? Is an Israeli child born more resilient than, say, a Mexican, an American, or anyone else? That is a good question that we are not prepared to weigh in on. If you have come this far in the book, you will have learned that Israelis come in every shape, size, and background, as evidenced by the range of people we interviewed. But environment does matter. Israel has a paucity of oil and natural gas, a deficit of neighboring allies, and innumerable national challenges to face, but Israelis do seem to have an innate resilience that is actively honed by the society they grow up in. The key is in the keys.

You will have noticed a thread that flows through the personal stories of each and every one of the people we profile in this book. They all embody and exemplify one of the ISResilience keys that we outlined at the beginning of this journey:

Empathy. It is the interpersonal skills, the inner strength, and the community of support that allowed Israel Meir Lau to survive the Nazis, arriving on the shores of Israel as a child orphan refugee and becoming the spiritual leader of Israel. It is the emotional heart of Sherri Mandell and her ability to share her feelings both in written and spoken word that transforms unbearable grief into a promise to ease the pain of others. It is Yoseph Haddad's sympathy for the sensitivities of others while overcoming personal death threats as he expresses his voice as an Arab citizen of the Jewish State of Israel. It is Miri Eisin's compassionate voice as she overcame the odds to break through barriers, becoming a colonel in the Israel Defense Forces and representing her nation to the world.

Flexibility. It is the motivation of Noam Gershony to change his direction mid-course, dedicating himself to a new goal after falling from the sky, beating death, and finally emerging an Olympic hero. It is the guts that Nadav Ben Yehuda demonstrates when forgoing reaching the peak of Mount Everest in order to save a life. It is overcoming a profound disability, the result of a freak accident with the potential to ruin your life, and using that as a jumping-off point to pioneer technology helping paraplegics walk again, as did Dr. Amit Goffer. It is Tal Brody giving up the opportunity to play in the NBA, in order to take a tiny country to basketball glory and in doing so, putting it on the sports map of the world to stay.

Meaning-making. It is the persistence of Brigadier-General Avigdor Kahalani moving forward after sustaining burns over 90 percent of his body, leading his troops to victory in battle and going on to live a life of service. It is the single-mindedness of Gadi Yarkoni to recover from having limbs blown off and win high office in order to better the life of his community. It is the grit and determination of Gadeer Kamal Mreeh to refuse to have others in her community define what a woman could achieve. It is the perseverance of the Zinati family, holding on to their traditions and identity at all cost, embodied in the last Jew in her town, Margalit. It is the relentless focus on the goal of reaching Jerusalem that led Shula Mola and Mequnante Rahamim to walk barefoot from Ethiopia, through the desert to the Promised Land. It is the fortitude and willpower of Natan Sharansky to survive years of solitude in the Soviet Gulag and emerge a human rights icon because he stood his ground for what is right.

These three keys: empathy, flexibility, and meaning are not exclusive. All of our interviewees express all of these keys to a greater or lesser degree. Each one of them exhibited the flexible and adaptive approach to life that is so integral to a resilient outlook. Flexibility means not only the ability to change direction mid-course. It also refers to the ability to touch the trauma, experience the pain and sadness, talk about the loss, yet be able in the next moment to experience joy, happiness, and excitement. This particular skill to move back and forth among a myriad of often conflicting and strong emotions is characteristic of each one of our interviewees and may be the single most important component of resilience.

Often there are additional factors that play into the resilient approach to life exhibited by the people we interviewed. Yet focusing on these three keys can provide a window for us into understanding the nature of resilience and help us to reflect on how these keys play out in our own lives.

Our interviewees are inspiring people who shed light on each one of the keys to resilience by the exemplary way they have lived their lives. Were they born that way? Were they raised that way? The answer to both those questions is most probably yes. But one thing is for certain. They all adopted a resilient mindset, which gave them the strength they needed to move forward and succeed. This resilient mindset is characteristic of Israeli society at large. Israelis are inculcated with a can-do attitude, expecting success, with no challenge too great to overcome. Israel's greatest natural resource is its people, as we have shown over the course of this book.

So what can you take from this book? Resilience can be a part of your life as well. Each one of us faces setbacks and adversity. We all have the ability to turn lemons into lemonade. The question is, how? The next time you are challenged, when an obstacle is placed in your path, when you are feeling lost or overcome by the circumstances you are confronting, recall the three keys to staying strong and moving ahead – empathy, flexibility, and meaning-making – and remember the people that embody ISResilience.

About the Authors

Michael Dickson

Michael Dickson is Executive Director of StandWithUs-Israel, an international educational nonprofit dedicated to supporting Israel and fighting antisemitism around the world. Michael regularly addresses audiences and broadcasts on issues pertaining to Israel and public diplomacy. He is an accomplished writer, with many published articles and TV appearances. Michael has addressed audiences in global forums, including at the UN, in the Knesset, and in Europe, America, Asia, and Africa.  Michael is a Senior Fellow at the Center for International Communication of Bar-Ilan University, is an honorary member of Alpha Epsilon Pi, and in 2015 was appointed to the Spectrum Forum of leading Executive Directors in Israel under the age of forty. In 2016, he was listed as the fourteenth most influential Jew on Twitter and also named in the "30 Israelis Making a Difference" at a special event at the President's Residence. Michael was listed in the top thirty of the *Jewish News*-Jewish Agency Aliyah 100 list of British immigrants to Israel as one of the "flag bearers who shape the State of Israel and made a significant contribution." In 2019, he was awarded the Bonei Zion ("Builder of Zion") Prize, recognizing the achievements of outstanding Anglo immigrants and their contribution to the State of Israel, at a ceremony in the Tower of David, Jerusalem. In 2020, he was listed on the Global Jewish 100, "a celebration of people across the world who are moving Jewish culture forward, selected according to their accomplishments, influence, and impact." He lives in Israel with his wife and five children.

Dr. Naomi L. Baum

Naomi L. Baum, PhD, is a psychologist who consults both in Israel and internationally in the field of trauma and resilience. She received her MA and PhD from Bryn Mawr College and her BA from Bar-Ilan University. Naomi created the Building Resilience Intervention (BRI), an evidence-based resilience model that has been applied widely in Israel and abroad. She was Director of the Resilience Unit at Metiv – The Israel Psychotrauma Center for twelve years and directed the International Course in Trauma and Resilience in cooperation with the Rothberg School of the Hebrew University. She trained with the Center for Mind-Body Medicine (CMBM) from 2004 to 2006 and is a member of their international faculty. In 2015 Naomi developed a multi-year post-trauma intervention in collaboration with Tevel b'Tzedek and helped to train staff and implement it in Nepal. She has worked with CMBM in Sonoma County, California, in the wake of the forest fires that swept that area. She is the author of professional articles on resilience building and trauma as well as several books, including *My Year of Kaddish: Mourning, Memory and Meaning*, published in April 2020; *Life Unexpected: A Trauma Psychologist Journeys through Breast Cancer*; and *Free Yourself from Fear: The Seven Day Plan for Overcoming Fear of (Recurrent) Cancer*. She is also a student and instructor of Qi Gong, a meditative form of movement based on the principles of Chinese medicine. She has been married to the same man for forty-five years and is mother of seven and grandmother of twenty.

Acknowledgments

Writing this book has been a labor of love and a small testimony to the significance that Israel, our homeland, has in the lives of my family. We are blessed to live in this time and to be able to live in this place.

My love and thanks to my childhood sweetheart, my best friend, and my wife (all one and the same person), Deborah, and to our beautiful children Dalia, Yoav, Yael, Dan, and Ella.

I am overwhelmed by the number of people who have played such a significant role in my life and who have been kind enough to encourage the genesis of this book. So lucky am I that my fear is that I will forget to mention people. With that disclaimer, I will do my best.

To my parents, Ruth and Stuart Dickson, thank you for imbuing me with a sense of love for my heritage, for my people, for society in general, and for our homeland. To my parents-in-law, Diane and Paul Kutner, I cherish your advice and encouragement. I must also thank my ever-kvelling brother and sister, Jonathan and Rachel, for their support. May the memory of my grandparents Renee and Woolf Isenberg and Jenny and David Dickson be a blessing; I remember them always.

I am dedicating my writing to Leah Silverman, my sister-in-law, who has been the model of resilience as she continues to overcome the setback of injury.

My wholehearted thanks to my coauthor Dr. Naomi Baum for her wisdom and professional insight. One of the first people I interviewed for this book (a number of years ago!) was Naomi, due to her extensive experience in this field, and I am grateful to her for agreeing to join me on this journey of discovery of a people and a country that we both love. She has achieved so much in the field of resilience and has been a wonderful writing partner.

I am lucky that my job is also my passion: I am blessed to have been part of the StandWithUs leadership team for fourteen years. My admiration and respect go to StandWithUs CEO Roz Rothstein for her leadership as well as her faith in me, which allowed me to be in a position to shine a light on the real Israel. I extend my appreciation to Roz's fellow StandWithUs cofounders Jerry Rothstein and Esther Renzer for your vision, commitment, and consistent support.

Thanks to my stellar team in Jerusalem as well as colleagues internationally, both present and past. I am blessed to work with such an array of talent. Particular thanks to my right-hand woman Shany Lousky-Levy, to my talented Associate Director Tamir Oren, and to Ilana Sherrington-Hoffman and Charlotte Korchak (with whom I always love to engage on books we read and ideas we have), as well as to the talented Paul Gorbulski, Noam Koren, Noa Raman, and Avigail Messika for their help and encouragement. Thank you to the exceptional Moran Reijzer for the cover art and for all his wonderful graphic design. Thank you to the students, activists, and global staff of StandWithUs who touch lives every day in an enduring fight against antisemitism with their dedication to bring people worldwide closer to Israel.

There are leaders in the Jewish world whom I have come to appreciate so much; they include the wonderful Debbie and Naty Saidoff; Rita and Steve Emerson; Adam and Gila Milstein; the late Newton Becker, z"l; Dahlia and Art Bilger; Nancy and Harry Bloomfield; Loretta and Perry Cash; Haim and Helen Dayan; Barbara Diamond; Jonty Feldman; Sharon and Larry Finegold; Motti Gur; Janice and Steve Hefter; Larry Hochberg; Alan Howard; Marty and Susan Jannol; Andrew Kligerman; Bruce Lederman; Dina and Fred Leeds; Barak Lurie; Alon and Rosana Miller; Tamara Morgenstern; Janet and

David Polak; Larry Post; Barak Raviv; Sheri Ross; Susy Rubenstein; Janet Sasson; Faith Schames; Peggy Shapiro; Rhona Wacht; Sonya and Howard Waldow; Adrienne and Michael Wienir; Barry Wolfe; Joy Wolfe MBE; Sylvan Adams and Evelyn and Dr. Shmuel Katz (Shmuel, you are a mentor whom I so admire).

Many extraordinary and inspiring people have advised me during this project, and others have been kind enough to give feedback on this work: special thanks to Senator Joe Lieberman, Rabbi Lord Jonathan Sacks, Professor Gil Troy, Ambassador Gilad Erdan, Ambassador Ron Prosor, Minister Orit Farkash Hacohen, Yossi Klein Halevi, Isaac Herzog, Daniel Gordis, David Horovitz, Einat Wilf, Yael Eckstein, Yaakov Katz, William Daroff, Aviva Klompas, Arsen Ostrovsky, and Joe Hyams. Thanks also to Sheryl Sandberg, the coauthor of *Option B: Facing Adversity, Building Resilience, and Finding Joy*, for her leadership on this issue and for her encouragement.

It was important for us to publish with an Israeli publisher. Thank you to Ilan Greenfield, CEO of Gefen Publishing House, for believing in this book and including it in a family of incredible literature. Our thanks go to you and to the entire team in Jerusalem and New York, especially to Project Manager Daphne Abrahams and to Senior Editor Kezia Raffel Pride for wise and incisive input.

To the wonderful people who agreed to be interviewed for this book and in doing so share their life lessons for us all to learn from, thank you. There are so many more stories of ISResilience to be inspired by; I pledge to continue telling them.

Michael Dickson
Jerusalem, August 2020

It is always a great pleasure to reach the stage of acknowledgements. First, great thanks to my coauthor Michael Dickson for his vision, inspiration, and invitation to work with him on this book. It was an honor and a privilege to meet so many outstanding individuals and to get a chance to have some wonderful conversations with them. Working with Michael has led me to appreciate his sincerity and drive, his ability to connect with people, and above all, what a mensch he is. What a pleasure it has been. In addition, his support staff was more than helpful in arranging for the many interviews that form the backbone of this book. Thank you all.

Thanks to my life partner, Mike, for always being ready to listen, support, and be an all-around best friend, and to my kids, all seven of them, who are my most loving critics. Thanks to the folks at Gefen for the encouragement and hard work to make this the final product it is.

And finally, I second Michael's thanks to our interviewees, the wonderful people who not only made time for us in their busy lives, but opened their homes, their hearts, and their souls to our probing and sometimes difficult questions. They taught us so much, and I am humbled and grateful to be able to share some of what we experienced with you, the reader.

Naomi Baum
Jerusalem, August 2020